UKE CAN DO IT!

UKE CAN DO IT!

DEVELOPING
YOUR SCHOOL
UKULELE PROGRAM

Philip Tamberino

Published in partnership with
NAFME: National Association for Music Education

ROWMAN & LITTLEFIELD
Lanham • Boulder • New York • Toronto • Plymouth, UK

Published in partnership with NAFME: National Association for Music Education

Published by Rowman & Littlefield
4501 Forbes Boulevard, Suite 200, Lanham, Maryland 20706
www.rowman.com

10 Thornbury Road, Plymouth PL6 7PP, United Kingdom

British Library Cataloguing in Publication Information Available

Library of Congress Cataloging-in-Publication Data

Tamberino, Philip, author.
  Uke can do it! : developing your school ukulele program / Philip Tamberino.
    pages cm
  Includes index.
  ISBN 978-1-4758-0415-7 (cloth : alk. paper) — ISBN 978-1-4758-0416-4
(pbk. : alk. paper) — ISBN 978-1-4758-0417-1 (electronic) 1. Ukulele—Instruction
and study. 2. School music—Instruction and study—United States. I. Title.
  MT801.U4T36 2014
  787.8'9071—dc23   2013046455

Printed in the United States of America

Dedicated with love to my grandfather, Philip Tamberino (1914–2005),
a true lover of the ukulele and believer in education.

CONTENTS

CONTENTS

PREFACE

When I first proposed a classroom ukulele program for a pilot class of third graders in my school, it was a new frontier for me and the school alike. Not only had it never been done in my district, no one was familiar with it being done anywhere else. Third graders were supposed to learn the recorder. I had never heard the ukulele mentioned in my teacher training or in any of the professional journals I read. The school music program supply catalogs that inundated my mailbox over the summer did not even advertise ukuleles at the time. And mentioning the ukulele to anyone over a certain age almost always prompted a reference to Tiny Tim.

Fortunately, the ukulele was not so obscure to me. I knew it from my childhood, from experiences listening to my grandfather singing and playing it in his reclining chair that I will never forget. He had enjoyed it as a pastime from his own childhood and continued playing into his nineties. In my own life experience up to that point, the ukulele had not been treated as a "serious" instrument in popular culture, but any instrument that could endear itself to a person for that long was "serious" to me in the best way possible.

As a new teacher, I thought about my grandfather playing the ukulele both as a boy and as a senior citizen, and I began to wonder why students could not learn the ukulele in school. It seemed ideal: They could sing and play at the same time, they could play chords or melodies or rhythm, it was virtually impossible to make an offensive sound with it, and it didn't require any special sizing for even the youngest children. Moreover, the ukulele seemed to have features that might shield it from the high attrition rates of many other school instruments: It was not costly to own, it was just as satisfying to play alone as with others, and it could be taken and practiced almost anywhere or anytime. In studying the ukulele and researching the topic, I concluded there was no better instrument to satisfy the interests of students and the music program alike.

The school supported me in piloting a classroom-based program, and with no materials for classroom ukulele readily available at the time, I developed my own. Before long the students were playing songs, teaching each other new chords, and even composing their own music. Families and staff delighted at the sight and sound of small children playing what looked like small guitars at that first spring concert, and the ukulele became a permanent part of the program thereafter. Community interest in the ukulele was piqued as well, prompting the creation of an adult education course with the school board president, school nurse, reading specialist, district clerk, and community members on the roster.

Throughout that period I wondered why the ukulele seemed so completely off the radar of the school districts in my area (if not most areas outside the Pacific states). New York was far away from Hawaii, but so were Canada, New Zealand, and the United Kingdom—all places, I learned, that had successful programs of various scale. This was not a new idea in music education, in fact its success seemed to have been replicated several times over. Convinced that the problem was only a lack of awareness and support, I sought opportunities to promote the use of the ukulele in schools to other music teachers and students beyond my own district. Again, the reception was strong, especially among preservice and younger in-service teachers who had fewer preconceptions about the instrument or who had already began playing on their own. This book is essentially an outgrowth of presentations and workshops I conducted to that end.

Much has changed for the ukulele in recent years, both in popular culture and music education. More people have heard the instrument—in chart-topping songs, viral videos, movies, or television commercials. With ukulele sales having boomed, more people know someone who actually owns a ukulele. Those school music catalogs now have whole pages devoted to ukuleles of multiple brands and styles. More music teachers are now aware of the ukulele having appeal among students, and the idea of using it in a school music program seems less esoteric. Tiny Tim is no longer the common point of reference, rather it is current music, movies, advertising, or even friends and family members.

This is a ripe time for the ukulele—partly because of its rise in status and partly because so many teachers have yet to lend their talents to it in an educational setting. There is, nonetheless, much work that remains to be done to support ukulele teaching in schools at anything near the level of more established types of music education. Even if it remains trendy and popular for some time, it is unlikely that school boards throughout America will suddenly clamor for ukulele instruction in their schools. Likewise, ukulele pedagogy is not likely to become required coursework for preservice teachers on a widespread basis anytime soon. Meanwhile, the growth of ukulele programs will continue to come from individual music educators who want to try something different, reach more students, make more connections to the world beyond school, or who simply love the instrument. For those people, I hope this book will be a helpful resource.

ACKNOWLEDGMENTS

I would like to thank the many people who have supported me as a music teacher and likewise the larger project of promoting the ukulele as a teaching tool in music education, including Principals Wendell Chu, Rosalia Bacarella, and Loretta Ferraro, Kenneth Schwartzman, Ruth Breidenbach and the NYSSMA Classroom Music Committee, Jennifer Miceli and the LIU Post chapter of NAfME Collegiate, and everyone at Rowman & Littlefield and NAfME who worked to make this book into a finished product. I would also have very little to say on the topic of ukulele education without the students from whom I continue to learn so much.

My family has always been a rock of support and likely shaped the underpinnings of this book in ways I probably will never completely understand or appreciate. I have to thank my parents especially for a lifetime of example both as teachers and as human beings. I am also forever grateful to my wife Daisy, not only for creating space in our lives for writing a book but for the real ways she has made this book—as well as my life—better by her being there.

INTRODUCTION

There is hardly a good reason why the ukulele should not be a fixture in American music education today. Few people—music educators included—are able to resist its charms, and it far surpasses the potential of any other single instrument as a practical learning tool. It is less expensive than the guitar or keyboard, more versatile than the recorder or xylophone, and less dependent on ensembles than band or orchestral instruments, to name a few plusses. Yet ukulele programs are currently few and far between when compared to other forms of music education.

Where ukulele programs do exist, they tend to be wildly successful, turning many students on to the joy of making music and, with any luck, creating lifetime music lovers. These programs have often been started by teachers who were already ukulele enthusiasts in some way and therefore had resources to draw on in developing their program. But for interested teachers with less background, the necessary support has been difficult to find through the traditional channels of teacher education programs and professional organizations. This book seeks to provide tools to help teachers realize the potential of the ukulele in their own program for their own ends and regardless of their prior experience.

Given the challenge of starting any new program potentially from scratch, a substantial part of this book (part I) covers practical topics associated with turning a ukulele program from an idea into a reality. It begins with obtaining a ukulele and becoming literate in the instrument, and it also covers making a successful pitch for administrative support and approaches to securing instruments for students. Part II covers aspects of the classroom environment and student learning with the ukulele, including classroom management techniques particular to the ukulele classroom, a general technical sequence for the instrument, and possible applications in both classroom and ensemble performance settings.

The content overall is organized in a sequence that reflects how a program would develop, from teacher learning first to student performance last. Since it takes much longer to bring a ukulele program from scratch to fruition than to read any book, the book is designed to facilitate revisiting and skipping around to information on an as-needed basis. Chapter headings and subheadings are as descriptive as possible, and an index of topics is also included to make specific information easy to find. Finally, a glossary, chord guide, scales, and beginner song suggestions are all included for reference.

The entire process covered here may take many months of dedicated work, but the reward is great and your students—in their own way—will thank you for it!

I

GETTING STARTED

1

OVERVIEW

Beloved throughout the world for its charm and accessibility, the ukulele is also one of the most ideal instruments for the teaching and learning of music. Few other instruments, if any, meet so many of the needs of both students and teachers and also possess as far-reaching appeal. From public beaches in Hawaii to the Royal Albert Hall in London, from street kids in Jakarta to CEOs like Warren Buffett, from Bach to bluegrass, the ukulele transcends matters of age, gender, wealth, style, and culture. Its strength comes from a versatility that not only makes it adaptable to many different kinds of music but different lifestyles and aptitudes as well. This gives it tremendous advantages in developing both music literacy and an affinity for music-making that can last a lifetime.

WHAT IS THE UKULELE?

The ukulele (fig. 1.1) is a four-stringed fretted instrument, similar to the guitar in form but significantly smaller and entirely pitched in the treble clef. Its tuning (g_4, c_4, e_4, a_4) is the same as the highest four strings of the guitar transposed up a perfect fourth, though the ukulele commonly features a "re-entrant" fourth string, which is tuned one octave up. This unique tuning, in conjunction with its size and the tradition of strumming it by hand (without a pick), gives the ukulele a characteristically light and breezy sound that is as enchanting when played by a master as it is forgiving when played by a beginner.

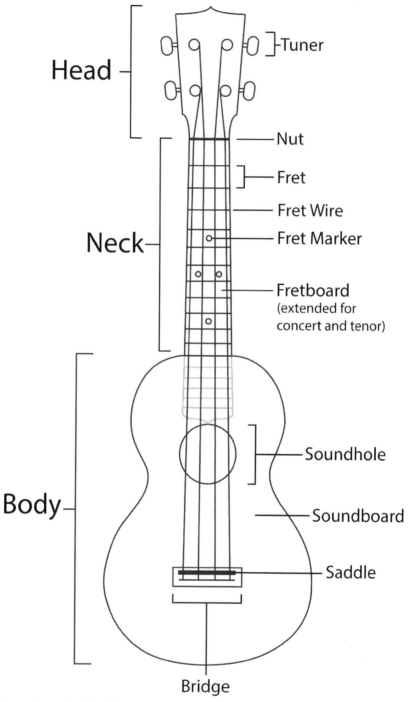

Head

Neck

Body

Tuner

Nut

Fret

Fret Wire

Fret Marker

Fretboard
(extended for
concert and tenor)

Soundhole

Soundboard

Saddle

Bridge

Figure 1.1. The Ukulele

The ukulele has a long-standing association with Hawaii, where it has been an integral part of the culture since its invention there in the late nineteenth century. Pronounced "oo-koo-LEH-leh" in Hawaiian, the ukulele was actually an invention of Portuguese immigrants to the island, who combined features of two other instruments to create what we now know as the ukulele. The ukulele became incorporated into traditional Hawaiian music soon after its invention and remains a part of both traditional and contemporary Hawaiian music performance today.

The ukulele has historically been popular among amateurs and professionals alike, and the current ukulele renaissance is no exception. Songs like "Somewhere Over the Rainbow/What a Wonderful World," and "Hey, Soul Sister" have brought the sound of the ukulele to tens of millions of people all over the world while sales of the instrument have soared to new heights. In addition to Hawaiian music, ukulele performance now spans genres including jazz, rock/pop, folk, classical, and even bluegrass, and remains an expanding area of innovation.

WHERE CAN THE UKULELE FIT IN SCHOOLS?

The ukulele is suitable for both classroom and ensemble purposes and is most efficient in use with students in grades 3 and up (although students as young as five years old are capable of playing the ukulele properly). Most students with special needs can also benefit tremendously from the ukulele, excepting only those with the most severe cases of motor impairment.

In a classroom setting, each student can use their own ukulele as a hands-on tool in learning concepts in the general music curriculum, including music theory, ear training, improvisation, and composition. While many instruments can be used for this purpose, the ukulele has a particularly gentle learning curve and much can be accomplished with very little technical skill. Where guitar or orchestral strings programs exist, the ukulele can also serve as an introductory stringed instrument. Likewise, the ukulele may be adapted for use in traditional classroom approaches to music education such as Orff Schulwerk or Dalcroze Eurhythmics.

In an ensemble setting, students can focus more on mastering the technique of the instrument and playing more complex arrangements. Homogeneous ukulele ensembles may accompany choral groups, sing and strum on their own, or play orchestral-style arrangements, while individual ukulele students may be part of smaller heterogeneous musical groups.

In any educational setting the ukulele has benefits that, taken together, no other single instrument has: it is affordable, portable, gentle-sounding, well-suited for melody and harmony *and* rhythm, technically simple for beginners, able to be played while singing, and enjoyable as a solo *or* ensemble instrument.

WHY INCLUDE THE UKULELE IN MUSIC EDUCATION?

Ukulele programs can get more students making music in school and, most importantly, offer them a viable path for continued music-making once they have graduated.

In school, the ukulele may attract students not reached by traditional instrumental offerings such as band and orchestra, given its stylistic versatility and crossover appeal. Younger students can also enjoy the prestige of playing a "grown-up" instrument in the music classroom, as there are no special sizes or design modifications necessary for children. The gentle learning curve of the ukulele and the homogeneous nature of a ukulele ensemble also make it easier to offer opportunities for beginners in later grades and thus help prevent instrumental music from being like a "ship that has sailed" for inexperienced older students.

Beyond school, the ukulele is highly compatible with the variables of life—such as having enough money, time, privacy, opportunities to play, etc.—that, with many other instruments, often result in even the most accomplished students letting music-making fall by the wayside. The ukulele, by contrast, can be conveniently taken almost anywhere, given its small size and light weight, and practiced almost anywhere without disturbing others, given its quiet sound. It stands well on its own as a solo instrument, not reliant on ensembles for satisfying performance experiences, though it remains well-suited for social settings and small-group music-making. *And* it does not cost very much to own.

Just as there are "lifetime sports," the ukulele may be considered a "lifetime instrument." While it may seem to music educators that all instruments are lifetime instruments, the reality is that some instruments offer certain opportunities—in terms of cost, convenience, and career—that others do not, and for some this can mean the difference between a life that includes playing an instrument and one that does not. If the goal is for all students to become educated listeners, performers, and creators of music, instruments like the ukulele can help more students believe that music really *is* for everybody.

2

BECOMING
UKULELE LITERATE

Prior to proposing any kind of school program to bring the ukulele to students, the teacher must be sufficiently literate in the ukulele her/himself. Ukulele literacy includes not only being able to play the instrument and read certain specialized notation, but having an awareness of how instruments may vary, the history of the instrument and its significant contributors, and the most relevant musical literature. Finally it includes knowing how to find the best opportunities for future learning.

GETTING YOUR OWN UKULELE

Ready to play? The journey toward a school ukulele program of course begins with a teacher having a ukulele. If it seems that there is any feasibility of the school district contributing to the cost of instruments at a later point, the teacher may try to get the school to purchase one ukulele as a demo of what students may eventually play. Borrowing one is fine as well, but ukuleles are not expensive to own, nor are they difficult to learn (for music teachers especially), so purchasing a ukulele prior to learning how to play carries rather low risk of buyer's remorse. If anything, it is likely to be the beginning of a beautiful friendship!

Trying Out Ukuleles

The best way to shop for a ukulele is to simply go to music stores and play as many ukuleles as possible. The point is to get an idea of what is available in terms of sizes, tone qualities, and price points. Ask a salesperson (or bring a ukulele-playing friend) to play a few licks on different models so you can better compare. A visit to a local music store is also a good opportunity to lay the groundwork for the purchase of a quantity of instruments or accessories down the road. See chapter 3 for information about ukuleles for students.

The main concern with any ukulele should be intonation. A ukulele that cannot stay in tune with itself is basically useless. To test intonation, first make sure all of the open strings are perfectly tuned (have a salesperson do this with an electronic tuner if necessary), then test each fretted note by pressing on the strings between the fret wires and plucking the string (don't worry about your technique at this point). There should be a difference in pitch of one half-step between each fret. Good intervals to check for intonation against the open strings are the octave (12th fret), perfect fifth (7th fret), and minor second (1st fret). If any of these intervals are noticeably out of tune, or if any fretted notes buzz or yield the same pitch as their neighbor, look for a different instrument to purchase.

If ukuleles are not available to try firsthand, it is certainly worth shopping through the Internet. Generally, this should only be done through a well-established dealer for the purchase of a well-established brand. Some sites actually feature video or audio clips of the ukulele being played, which can give a general sense of its tone quality. In any case, free or low-cost return shipping is advisable!

Understanding Ukulele Product Descriptions

Ukuleles are commercially described both by their size and the wood from which they are principally made. There are three common sizes for ukuleles: *soprano*, *concert*, and *tenor* (fig. 2.1). Soprano is the smallest, followed by concert, and then tenor.

These sizes all use the same tuning and differ only in tone quality, range, and cost (which generally increases along with size). Sopranos were originally the only size available and thus tend to be associated with a classic Hawaiian sound. Concert ukuleles were invented later to allow for more

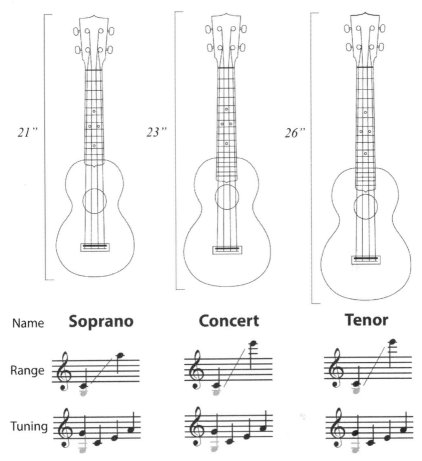

Figure 2.1. Common sizes for ukuleles

projection but still preserve the light character of the soprano. Tenors offer a more resonant sound and are favored among professionals today. Keep in mind that many adults—even those with thick fingers or large hands—play soprano ukuleles, and even young children can play the larger sizes as well.

The wood is also a selling point for ukuleles because of how the composition of the body affects the tone quality, volume, and sustain of the instrument. Woods may either be a "laminate" (a layer of fine wood on top of inferior wood), or a uniform piece of "solid" wood, with solid wood being the higher quality choice. Because of the different roles they play in determining the sound, the top face of the ukulele (the soundboard) may

> ## WHAT ABOUT THE BARITONE UKULELE?
>
> For the purposes of this book, the baritone ukulele is treated separately from the other sizes. Larger yet than the tenor ukulele, the body of a baritone is equivalent to a half-sized guitar. And while the baritone still has four strings like other ukuleles, they are also tuned like the highest four strings of the guitar (d_3 g_3 b_3 e_4). As a result, the location of any given chord or note will be different on the baritone fretboard than on other ukuleles.
>
> If you buy a baritone ukulele, you can have the dealer specially string it to be pitched the same as other ukuleles. Otherwise, the teacher should not purchase a baritone ukulele unless teaching students the baritone ukulele.

be made of a different wood than the back and sides. Some woods, such as *spruce*, are only used for tops, while others, such as *mahogany*, may be used for the entire body.

The premium wood for ukuleles has always been *koa*, which yields a very warm and sweet tone. Because koa is indigenous to Hawaii, and therefore scarce, solid koa ukuleles are the most expensive on the market. *Mahogany* is more common in mid-range ukuleles because it produces a similarly distinctive sound but is a more readily available material. More obscure woods such as *agathis* and *nato* are common in starter ukuleles because they are less expensive yet but still give a fairly warm tone. *Maple* is also common in starter ukuleles but offers a significantly brighter/drier sound, along with *bamboo*.

While not necessarily a selling point, another variation between ukuleles is the tuning mechanism. Ukuleles may feature geared or "machine-head" tuners (like a guitar) or the more traditional friction peg tuners (like a violin). Geared tuners make tuning easier by giving the knob a 14:1 turning ratio, meaning that full turns of the knob only adjust the tuning slightly. By contrast, friction pegs turn the knob at a 1:1 ratio, meaning that very small movements of the knob can alter the tuning substantially. By their nature, they are less susceptible to getting knocked out of tune accidentally but require a more precise touch than the more user-friendly geared tuner. For a teacher, it is ultimately a matter of personal preference. See chapter 3 for information on student ukuleles.

Keep It Simple, but Not Too Cheap

As a first-timer, you will be looking for a good "starter" ukulele. This is not necessarily the least expensive ukulele you can find, but a basic model that has a pleasing tone and is made well. The very lowest-priced ukuleles on the market are not likely to be of good quality, meaning that the instrument may not play in tune with itself, strings may buzz on the frets, or the bridge may snap off after a few months. Look for a ukulele with a plain wood finish and traditional ukulele shape (like a guitar)—no painted bodies, f-holes, pickups, elaborate fret markers, or any other frills are necessary. As you become a more experienced player, you can upgrade to a new instrument according to the more particular taste you will have developed (see "Next Steps" in this chapter).

BASICS OF PLAYING THE UKULELE

While becoming a true master of the ukulele prior to teaching students is ideal, it is neither necessary nor advisable if one hopes to begin a ukulele program in the near future. Rather, a music teacher may develop a skill level well ahead of beginning students in a relatively short period of time through self-teaching and regular practice. It then simply remains for the teacher to *continue* staying well ahead of students as they progress.

The information in this section is intended to help a teacher with no prior experience get started playing the ukulele but should be extended with the types of activities outlined at the end of the chapter. Chapter 6 also contains a skill learning sequence to direct future learning as well.

Tuning the Ukulele

The standard tuning for ukuleles is g_4, c_4, e_4, a_4 (fig. 2.2), with the strings numbered in order from *right to left* like the guitar and orchestral stringed instruments. Note that the third string (c) is the lowest pitch and the open strings together produce a root position C6 chord. Because there are alternative tunings possible for the ukulele, this tuning is referred to as "C6" tuning, with a "high fourth" or "high g" string. The lyrics "My dog has fleas" have traditionally been sung to the pitches played on the beat from fourth to first (g, c, e, a), as a device for remembering the sound of this tuning.

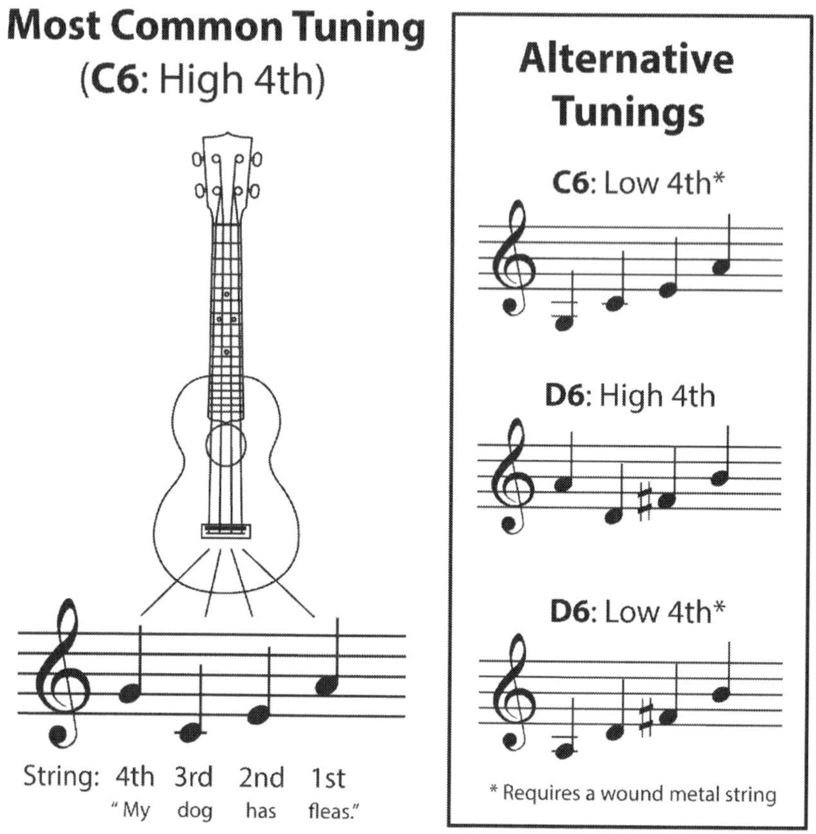

Most Common Tuning
(C6: High 4th)

String: 4th 3rd 2nd 1st
" My dog has fleas."

Alternative Tunings

C6: Low 4th*

D6: High 4th

D6: Low 4th*

* Requires a wound metal string

Figure 2.2. Ukulele tunings

There are four basic ways to tune a ukulele:

1. *Using an Electronic Tuner*—This is the most efficient method, in which a meter instantly tells the player how in-tune the note is. Internet websites have free tuners that can be used as long as the computer has a microphone. Small digital clip-on tuners specifically made for ukuleles can be set to "listen" only for the notes of a C6 or D6 tuned ukulele, to help avoid tuning to the wrong pitches.
2. *Using Reference Notes*—Pitch pipes, or the piano keyboard can provide the tones to match to each of the four strings. These require more use of the ear in matching pitch (fig. 2.3).

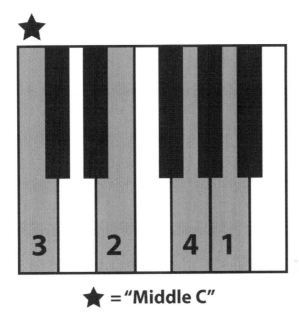

★ = "Middle C"

Figure 2.3. Using reference notes on the piano to tune the ukulele

3. *Using a Single Reference Note*—In this method, only one string is matched to a reference note (usually **a**) and the others are tuned based on that string. The reference note may come from another instrument or a tuning device such as a tuning fork. After tuning the **a** string to match the reference note, the second and fourth strings can then be tuned by fretting an **a** on each string and matching it to the open **a**. The open third string (**c**) can then be matched fretting an **e** and matching it to the open **e** string (fig. 2.4a).

4. *Tuning the Ukulele to Itself*—For those situations where there is no reference note available, those with "perfect pitch" or good relative pitch may tune the ukulele *to itself* based on the intervals between the strings (**g-c-e-a**: Descending P5, Ascending Major third, Ascending P4, respectively). Alternately, the **c** string may be used as a reference note and other strings tuned from there using the method below (fig. 2.4b).

Tuning to a Reference Note

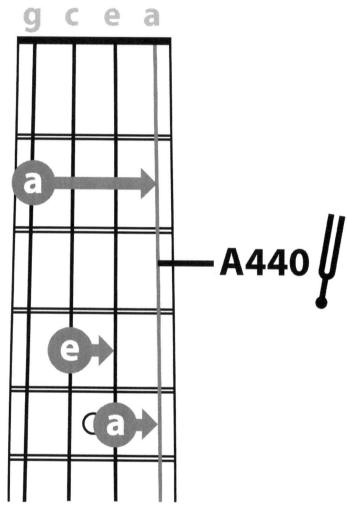

Figure 2.4a.   Open string a may be tuned with a tuning fork, then treated as a reference note for tuning other strings.

Tuning the Ukulele to Itself

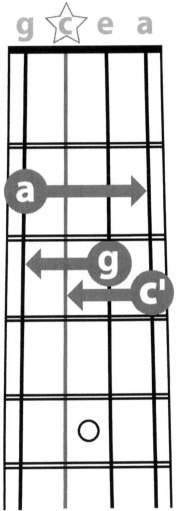

Figure 2.4b.   Open strings can be tuned to a fretted string according to the diagram. Open string c may be treated as a reference note.

Figure 2.5.   Playing position

Playing Position

The ukulele is held similar to the way one would cradle a baby, and the major parts of the instrument—"head," "neck," and "body"—support this analogy nicely (young children also find it amusing). Unless the ukulele is specially strung for a left-handed person, the left hand supports the neck, and the right forearm holds the body instrument flat against the center of the player's torso. The instrument should be secure such that you can stand up without it falling to the floor. The fingertips of the right hand should be approximately where the neck meets the body (the strumming area) and the instrument should be at about a 45 degree angle (fig. 2.5).

Strumming

The ukulele is traditionally strummed by hand, not with a pick. If a pick is ever used, it is a soft felt pick, not a hard pick as is used with guitars. Any chord can be played using all four strings, so it is never necessary to skip or deaden individual strings to play particular chords. To get the "sweetest"

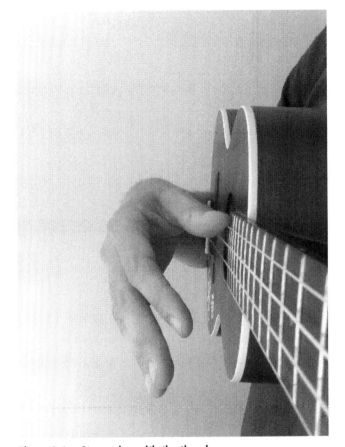

Figure 2.6. Strumming with the thumb

sound, the strings are strummed at their midpoint, which happens to be where the neck meets the body of the instrument. Note that this technique again differs from that of the guitar, which is strummed over the sound hole.

There are perhaps a dozen different ways to strum the ukulele, some of which involve all five fingers, but the simplest strum is to brush the strings with the outward side of the thumb in a downward motion (fig. 2.6).

A brighter and more versatile strum involves the index finger. The motion of the index finger strum is often described as beginning with pointing the finger to oneself, then flicking the wrist so the finger makes contact with all the strings, and finishing with the finger extended and pointing to the floor (fig. 2.7).

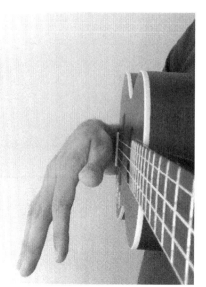

Figure 2.7. Strumming with index finger

Some people prefer to support the index finger with the thumb, as if holding a pick, though when attempting more advanced strums involving both the thumb and index finger this will not be possible. Likewise, to do multi-finger strums later on there can be no fingers curled up in the palm, so it is best to leave them loose from the beginning.

Fretting Notes and Chords

The technique for fretting notes on the ukulele is similar to other fretted instruments and involves pressing on the strings between the raised fret wires hard enough so that the string rings when strummed or plucked. When fingers reach over open strings, it is important that they create a "bridge" so they do not touch, and therefore deaden, other strings (fig. 2.8).

Pianists may need some time adjusting to ukulele finger numbering, which begins with the index finger as "1" and goes outward to the pinky as "4" (fig. 2.9).

The thumb requires no number because it is never used on the fretboard; however, it should consistently remain on the back of the neck to provide the opposable force necessary for applying good pressure to the strings. It also forces the hand into a position giving the fingers greater reach and leverage (fig. 2.10).

Figure 2.8. Creating a "bridge" over open strings.

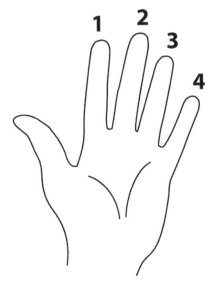

Figure 2.9. Left-hand (fretting hand) ukulele fingering.

Figure 2.10.   The thumb should remain on the back of the neck when fretting strings.

To accommodate different chord formations, the position of the hand may pivot from the wrist, but the arm and elbow should always remain relaxed.

Notation

Sheet music for the ukulele may be notated on the treble staff without transposition, but more specialized notation may be used to indicate fretting, fingering, and performance techniques particular to stringed instruments.

Ukulele chord diagrams indicate which frets to press in order to play a particular chord (fig. 2.11a). The diagram appears as a grid with the vertical lines representing the strings and the horizontal lines representing the fret

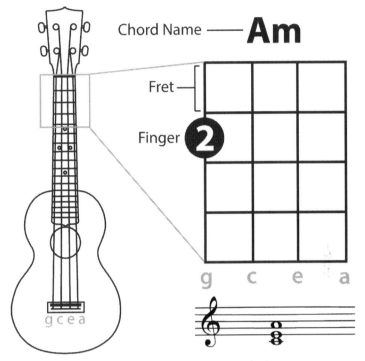

Figure 2.11a. Relation of the chord diagram to the instrument.

wires. The name of the chord appears at the top of the diagram, while black dots indicate where fingers should press the strings. Numbers inside or near the dots can be used to indicate *which* fingers to use for instructional purposes but are not typically included in commercial sheet music. When it is necessary to finger beyond the first four or five frets, one of the frets will be labeled with a number on the right of the diagram (fig. 2.11b).

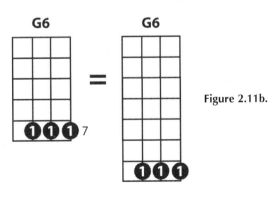

Figure 2.11b.

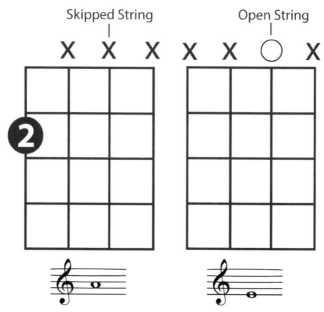

Figure 2.11c. Notation of individually picked strings on a chord diagram.

Chord diagrams may also be used to represent the fingering of individual notes, with skipped strings indicated by an "x" above the individual string and any open strings indicated with an "O" (fig 2.11c).

Chord diagrams are normally used in conjunction with treble staff notation in order to show duration and, in some cases, a strumming pattern. The diagram appears above the staff precisely when the chord is to begin being played. It is understood that the accompanying chord remains valid until a new chord diagram appears or the song ends. Therefore the diagram only appears once despite the fact that the chord may be strummed many times. The particular pattern for strums may be indicated in standard notation accompanied by "up" and "down" symbols like those used for violin bowing. See chapter 6 for common strumming patterns and a chord-learning sequence, and also the appendix for a more comprehensive list of chord diagrams.

Tablature is another way of showing where to fret strings but is more conducive to melodic passages. Four horizontal lines represent the four strings, and numbers are placed on the lines to indicate which fret to press (open strings are indicated with a "0"). Specific fingering for melodic passages can be indicated using letters (*p:* thumb, *i:* index, *m:* middle, *a:* ring, *c:*

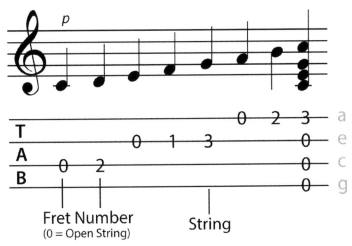

Figure 2.12. Tablature in relation to treble staff notation.

pinky). Chords simply appear as a vertical stack of numbers, indicating that all strings should be played at once. Like chord diagrams, tablature is also used in conjunction with standard notation to show the precise duration of notes as well as articulation.

LISTENING GUIDE

In practicing the ukulele, it is good to listen to examples of experienced performers for both recreation and inspiration. For an introduction to the use of the ukulele in different genres, consider the following playlists (as well as other tracks on the same album or by the same performer):

Popular Songs for Ukulele

Artist	Title	Album
Israel Kamakawiwo'ole	"Somewhere Over the Rainbow / What a Wonderful World"	Facing Future
Jason Mraz	"I'm Yours"	We Sing. We Dance. We Steal Things
Bruno Mars	"Count On Me"	Doo-Wops & Hooligans
Jake Shimabukuro	"While My Guitar Gently Weeps"	Gently Weeps
Train	"Hey Soul Sister"	Save Me San Francisco

Ukulele Jazz

Artist	Title	Album
Lyle Ritz	"Don't Get Around Much Anymore"	*How About Uke?*
Jake Shimabukuro	"Misty"	*Gently Weeps*
Herb Ohta ("Ohta-San")	"One Note Samba"	*Soul Time in Hawaii*
Bill Tapia	"Satin Doll"	*Livin' It Live*
Roy Smeck	"Five Foot Two"	*The Magic Ukulele of Roy Smeck*

Hawaiian Songs

Artist	Title	Album
Israel Kamakawiwo'ole	"Henehene Kou 'Aka"	*Facing Future*
Jesse Kalima	"Hilawe"	*Holiday in Hawaii*
Ka'au Crater Boys	"Noho Paipai"	*Valley Style*
Daniel Ho & Herb Ohta Jr.	"Kanaka Waiwai"	*Ukuleles in Paradise*
Eddie Kamae	"Aloha Oe"	*Heart of the Ukulele*

Singer-Songwriters

Artist	Title	Album
Colbie Caillat	"Tied Down"	*Coco*
Eddie Vedder	"Can't Keep"	*Ukulele Songs*
Sara Bareilles/Ingrid Michaelson	"Winter Song"	*Winter Songs*
Elvis Costello	"The Scarlet Tide"	*The Delivery Man*
Jack Johnson	"Breakdown"	*In Between Dreams*

Basically Bach

Artist	Title	Album
John King	Partita No. 3: I-VI (J.S. Bach)	Bach: Partita No. 3, BWV 1006
Jake Shimabukuro	"Two Part Invention No. 4 in D Minor" (J.S. Bach)	LIVE
Herb Ohta ("Ohta-San")	"Toccata and Fugue in D Minor" (J.S. Bach)	Ukulele Bach
John King	"Jesu Joy of Man's Desiring" (J.S. Bach)	Bach: Partita No. 3, BWV 1006
James Hill	One Small Suite for Ukulele: I-III (J. Hill)	A Flying Leap

Indie Ukulele

Artist	Title	Album
Beirut	"Elephant Gun"	Elephant Gun
Noah and the Whale	"5 Years Time"	Peaceful as the World Lays
Magnetic Fields	"Absolutely Cuckoo"	69 Love Songs
She & Him	"Turn to White"	Volume 3
Amanda Palmer	"Idioteque"	Performs the Hits of Radiohead on Her Magical Ukulele

WHO'S WHO?

Knowing the background of the instrument, its origins, development, and its most significant and innovative performers can help teachers connect the ukulele to other subject areas and communicate its value and relevance to students.

The first people to develop the ukulele in the 1880s were **Manuel Nunes** (1843–1922), **José do Espirito Santo** (1850–1905), and **Augusto Dias** (1842–1915), all emigrants to Hawaii from the Portuguese island of Madeira. They made their livings as woodworkers, crafting (and also playing) instruments like the Portuguese *machete* and *rajão*, which they effectively hybridized to create what became known as an *'ukulele* (meaning "jumping flea" in Hawaiian). From the *machete* the ukulele got its small size and four strings, and from the *rajão* it received its characteristic tuning.

King David Kalakaua (1836–1891) and **Queen Liliʻuokalani** (1838–1917), the last two reigning monarchs of the Kingdom of Hawaii, respectively, both played the ukulele and contributed to its initial popularity in Hawaiian culture. Liliʻuokalani even wrote her own songs for the ukulele, including the classic "Aloha Oe." Amid threats to Hawaiian sovereignty from foreign influences (like the United States), both monarchs viewed music and other cultural traditions as a unifying force among their people. The ukulele became incorporated into many rituals and ceremonies during this time, including the newly revived tradition of *hula*. Though Hawaii was ultimately annexed to the United States in 1898, the ukulele remains integral to Hawaiian musical traditions through today.

Outside Hawaii, ukulele popularity has ebbed and flowed many times since its invention, often affected by the advent of new media and trends in popular music. Following performances of Hawaiian music and dance at the 1915 world's fair in San Francisco (billed as the Panama-Pacific International Exposition), a ukulele craze swept the mainland United States through the 1920s. Major instrument manufacturers began producing ukuleles for the first time. It became a popular choice for amateurs and professionals alike and appeared in many popular Hawaiian-themed songs (authentic and otherwise). During this time new types of ukuleles were developed, including the concert, tenor, and baritone sizes, as well as the "pineapple" ukulele. In the sheet music of the day (a vital way of disseminating new music), ukulele chord diagrams were commonly included in popular songs.

With the advent of the radio, the first major stars of the ukulele emerged in the 1920s, including **Roy Smeck** (1900–1994) and **Cliff "Ukulele Ike" Edwards** (1895–1971). Later, in the 1930s and 1940s, the ukulele craze spread across the pond to the United Kingdom as comedian/musician **George Formby** (1904–1961) entertained audiences in films and live concerts. Following the turmoil of World War II, the ukulele and Hawaii itself again gained media attention. **Arthur Godfrey** (1903–1983), an influential personality on another new medium—television—contributed to a second wave of ukulele popularity in America through performances on his eponymous show, and in politics there began to be calls for Hawaiian statehood.

As the counterculture movement grew in the 1960s, along with the profile of rock music and the guitar, the ukulele fast became associated with dated musical styles or crossover Hawaiian fare from artists like **Don Ho**

(1930–2007). During this time, entertainer **Tiny Tim** (1932–1996) became synonymous with the ukulele for many Americans through his eccentric performances on the televised variety show *Laugh-In*. Despite its ostensible decline in relevance, some legendary rock guitarists of the time were known to have enjoyed the ukulele, including George Harrison and John Lennon of The Beatles, Pete Townshend of The Who, Brian May of Queen, and Joe Strummer of The Clash. Also around this time Canadian music administrator **J. Chalmers Doane** (b. 1938) began pioneering the use of ukulele in Nova Scotia schools (and later across Canada). Nevertheless, by the 1970s production of ukuleles had ceased in all but a few locations in the world, and the instrument was all but gone from American popular music.

Around the turn of the millennium, the tide began turning for the ukulele again. Nurtured by the growth of the Internet, the ukulele began enjoying a renaissance that included new stars, new music, and new ways of learning. **Israel Kamakawiwoʻole**'s (1959–1997) solo recording of "Somewhere Over the Rainbow / What a Wonderful World" (1993) was an important catalyst, with the song's licensing in film and television helping it garner worldwide commercial and critical success. At the same time, **John King** (1953–2009) effectively silenced any holdouts that the ukulele was not a "serious" instrument by arranging, performing, and recording works by J. S. Bach using authentic Baroque performance practices specially adapted for the ukulele. Later, King also (co-)authored the first scholarly book on the history of the ukulele (*The 'Ukulele: A History*). In 2006, **Jake Shimabukuro** (b. 1976) gained notoriety with an Internet video of his self-arranged solo instrumental performance of George Harrison's "While My Guitar Gently Weeps." As one of the earliest "viral" videos on YouTube, it reached more than four million viewers its first year (a high number for the nascent website) and introduced many people to a new sound and image for the ukulele. The Internet subsequently gave birth to a host of user-uploaded performance videos, tutorials, and meetups that continue to support people in learning the ukulele today.

NEXT STEPS

Having purchased a ukulele, developed basic playing skills, and become familiar with popular literature and the big names in ukulele history, there are several steps that can help bring one's enjoyment of the ukulele to the next level.

Participate in a local jam or community group—Many areas have informal performance opportunities available for ukulele enthusiasts. Often coordinated through the Internet, community groups may have regular meetings at places such as pubs, parks, or library public spaces in order to play for enjoyment. These groups are typically welcoming of anyone regardless of their level of talent, and people tend to be very willing to share their knowledge (and their sheet music) to help others. This type of setting offers an informal, social setting in which to learn by doing.

Attend a private lesson or group workshop—Often a master performer can offer students simple tips in technique that can dramatically alter the way they play (and teach) the ukulele. Being a learner in a formal setting also refreshes teachers' perspectives when coming back to their own classroom. Not all areas of the country have authentic ukulele teachers readily available, but it may be worth traveling a bit for the experience.

Attend a ukulele festival—Many states (and foreign countries) now have at least one recurring annual ukulele festival, often held in a metropolitan area. These events are a great opportunity to see accomplished ukulele performers, purchase ukuleles and related accessories, and attend workshops. Many also include support of ukulele in schools as part of their mission and feature student groups in performance. The best festivals, such as the Ukulele Festival Hawaii (since 1970), are free.

Upgrade your ukulele—With more playing experience comes more particular taste and sensitivity to the sound and feel of the instrument. While your first ukulele may remain your favorite, you may wish to try a ukulele of a different size or tone. A second ukulele is also a great way to experiment with alternative tunings without having to retune or restring your instrument repeatedly. If cost is a factor, simply purchasing higher-quality strings is a quick way to upgrade a starter ukulele.

3

STARTING A SCHOOL UKULELE PROGRAM

Starting a school ukulele program from scratch is an exciting opportunity to bring a new kind of music education to students. As with any kind of pioneering work, it is not without its challenges, but in overcoming them the rewards can be great. This chapter outlines a general path for starting a ukulele program at any level and of any scope.

WHAT IS YOUR GOAL?

The ukulele is versatile enough to be located in a variety of educational settings and serve a variety of ends, but it cannot begin everywhere at once and should not be introduced to a program without a specific focus. Ask the following questions when considering your goals in starting a ukulele program:

- Are there any deficiencies in the music program that a ukulele program could fill?
- Are there any (other) teachers on staff who already play the ukulele?
- Do I want students to have their own instrument?
- Will there be access to any funding?
- Which location(s) offer the greatest likelihood of success?
- What do I want students to get out of their experience with the ukulele?

The answers to questions like these will allow the teacher to pinpoint a specific level and scope for the program. Some possible locations of the ukulele in a music program include:

After-School Programs or Clubs

This is probably the best way to begin working with the ukulele in a school. It is generally easier to obtain a charter for an extra-curricular program than it is to begin modifying existing curricular programs. By its nature as a voluntary activity, an extra-curricular program is likely to attract only interested and motivated students, resulting in a smaller, more select group poised for higher achievement. Fewer instruments are necessary, and it may be feasible to make student ownership of instruments a requirement. The number of students admitted to the group—and even *which* students are admitted—may be at the discretion of the teacher. Such a group is altogether likely to move faster and accomplish more than a larger, more general population. The more self-contained setting can also provide the teacher with a better sense of how a particular school population might respond to a more expansive program. The group's performance(s) can also serve to put ukulele "on the map" and effectively set the stage for a wider use of the instrument in the music program at a later time.

Classroom Music

As a tool for developing music literacy per the curricular goals of classroom music, the ukulele can be of value to students of almost any age and any ability. Its greatest potential, however, is with regularly abled students from around age nine and up. This is because advancing on the ukulele involves fine-motor and cognitive skills that not all students readily possess at younger ages (although many do). Progress is simply slower with younger groups and students with special needs. See chapter 7 for a fuller exploration of the applications of the ukulele in a classroom setting.

Performing Ensembles

Whereas a classroom ukulele program is more focused on the ukulele as a teaching tool, a ukulele ensemble can focus more explicitly on developing mastery of the instrument itself. Students in elementary grades through high school can perform orchestral-style literature (written in parts, in standard notation), jazz literature (using lead sheets and featuring improvisation), or "sing-and-strum" literature, in which the group sings while accompanying themselves with chords. See chapter 8 for a fuller exploration of the ukulele in a performance setting.

Pre-Guitar

Guitar education has been a growing area of music education for several decades, though the instrument in its full size is a bit large for younger students. While the ukulele should not be considered simply a small guitar or "guitar lite," it can be an effective introduction to fretted stringed instruments in general. The four strings of the ukulele are tuned exactly one perfect fourth higher than the first four strings of the guitar, making some fingerings the same; however, the different number of strings does necessitate different techniques and allows for different musical possibilities between the two instruments.

Pre-Orchestra

The ukulele bears at least as much resemblance to orchestral stringed instruments as the recorder bears to wind band instruments and may hence serve to fill a "pre-orchestra" niche alongside its "pre-band" counterpart. With most orchestra programs beginning in fourth or fifth grade, and few students learning orchestral instruments as beginners at the secondary level, third grade or fourth grade classroom music would be the ideal setting for this purpose.

MAKING A PITCH

The powers that be are generally more receptive of proposals from people who have at least done their homework, so be sure to be prepared before approaching a supervisor about a ukulele program.

To promote the ukulele to people who may be unfamiliar with it or its benefits in music education, consider the following "top 10" talking points in a conversation about starting a ukulele program:

1. *It's Economical*—Ukuleles can cost less than a video game and are significantly less expensive than any other school instrument of similar capacity; students can own their own instrument easily both as children and later as adults.
2. *It's Versatile*—The ukulele can be used to play melody, chords, rhythm, or all at the same time, and you can sing and play at the same time; it has a demonstrated capacity for popular music, jazz, and classical music, among other styles.
3. *It's Rewarding for Beginners*—The ukulele has a gentle learning curve; it is possible to learn how to sing and play a song in a matter of minutes with no prior experience.
4. *It's the Right Size*—Children as young as first grade can form chords and make a sound, and there is no special sizing for children; adults can and do play the same sized instruments.
5. *It's Portable*—Ukuleles can weigh less than a pound and can be carried in cases about the size of a small backpack (which can themselves be worn as backpacks).
6. *It Has a Gentle Sound*—The ukulele is virtually incapable of making a loud or obnoxious sound; it can be practiced without disturbing others in a household; even "wrong" notes do not sound terribly dissonant.
7. *It's Both a Solo and Ensemble Instrument*—The ukulele can cover enough musical bases so as not to require any accompaniment; however, it is also adaptable to homogeneous or heterogeneous ensembles.
8. *It's Ideal for Learning Music Theory and Ear Training*—The ukulele is a chromatic, non-transposing instrument that is read on the treble staff and is particularly conducive to playing in the key of C—both a child-friendly key for singing and central key in music theory.
9. *It Has Popular Appeal*—The ukulele is reflected in life outside the classroom and has been featured in popular songs with which students may already be familiar.
10. *It's Cross-Cultural*—The ukulele is a hybrid of two Portuguese instruments, invented in Hawaii, popularized in the United States, and adopted by other countries including Japan, Great Britain, Canada, New Zealand, and Indonesia. The ukulele also shares common an-

cestry with similar Latin American instruments including the Brazilian *cavaquinho* and the Venezuelan *cuatro*.

Tailoring the pitch to the particular audience is important, and this can be accomplished by keeping in mind their unique interests, particularly when they are nonmusicians. A principal may not, for instance, appreciate the "chromatic" capabilities of the instrument, but s/he may respond to its relatively low cost. Parents might be interested in its quiet sound and portability. A school board might appreciate the uniqueness of the program and its potential to generate positive publicity for the school district. The one thing that most everyone will be interested in, however, will be the cost.

FUNDING AND PARENTAL INVOLVEMENT

It would seem reasonable to try to find or raise enough money to buy one class worth of instruments and keep them in school, but this actually misses out on many of the ukulele's key advantages. The instrument is small and light enough to be taken to and from school with ease, and it is also quiet enough to be practiced in almost any household without disturbing others. Without home practice students will make much slower progress. The ukulele is also inexpensive when compared with any other instrument of similar capacity and tends to cost less than many of the common trappings of student life—including phones, video games, and designer apparel—on which students or families already spend money. Student ownership of instruments not only provides them with an instrument for many years into the future but also gives them a greater stake in the program. Especially when school district money may be tight to begin with, it is worth exploring options that provide for buy-in from other source(s).

If parents will be asked to contribute to the cost, they need to be sold on the program just as a supervisor would. To simply send a letter home one day asking $50 for a ukulele and a case is not likely to be a winning strategy. Once a supervisor has cleared the way, presenting the idea on open school night, at a PTA meeting, or at least in an initial letter to families, is important to generate support. Any type of promotion should review a list of talking points about why the ukulele is so exceptional. Having enough skills to give a glittering demonstration of the instrument in front of a live audience helps (and if not, there are troves of high-quality video performances by the ukulelists mentioned in chapter 2 available on the Internet). Having ukuleles on hand for parents to try themselves can also increase interest, for many may have never even held one. Parents, wanting to give their children as many opportunities as possible and valuing music sometimes more than school districts do, will likely be receptive, and experienced parent leaders are likely to have the most practical ideas for funding and implementation. Once a program of any size has been established, student performances can be used to demonstrate the value or potential of the program as well.

The full exploration of opportunities for fundraising, grants, and even donated instruments is recommended, particularly if the school district and families alike are in dire straits. With a $1,000 grant, for instance, it is possible to provide enough ukuleles for a group of 20–25 students. If other parties contribute to the cost, it is possible to cover twice as many. Where possible, the teacher may even facilitate a buyback program (think college textbooks), where incoming students may purchase used instruments from outgoing classes. Ultimately, the aim should be to provide students with instruments, rather than the school, if at all possible.

GUIDELINES FOR STUDENT INSTRUMENTS

To the extent that the teacher has control over the types of ukuleles students play, it is best to keep classroom ukuleles as uniform as possible. If students are in a position to obtain their own instrument, the teacher may wish to issue certain guidelines to ensure the student's instrument will be appropriate for the setting in which it will be used (uniform tuning and stringing being the main concern). In any case, teachers should do their best to sell students on the ukulele itself, not necessarily a particular brand.

Quality

The primary considerations for a student ukulele should be intonation and durability, both of which are basically reflections of a brand's quality control. If the instrument cannot play in tune with itself, or if it falls apart after a few months, the instrument is effectively useless as an educational tool. It is common to experience quality control problems with the very lowest-priced ukuleles on the market. While their price may be initially attractive, the cost of repairs or replacements down the road can make them more expensive in the end. It is therefore advisable to spend a little extra for a reputable brand. Refer to chapter 2 for methods of testing a ukulele's intonation.

Sizes

One of the distinct advantages of a school ukulele program is that the instrument does not require special sizing for students of different ages. The soprano ukulele was once simply "the ukulele," before larger sizes were invented, and is played by children and adults alike all over the world. The fact that most soprano ukuleles have exactly twelve frets is perhaps the most advantageous for the music classroom, given the twelve tones of the chromatic scale (the last fret is the octave).

Tuning

The default tuning for most starter ukuleles from the factory, regardless of size, is C6 high-4th tuning, and this is a perfectly good choice for any new program. The centrality of the key of C in music theory supports the use of C6 tuning over D6 tuning in a music classroom, and although low-4th tuning has its advantages—such as organizing the strings in pitch order, expanding the range of the instrument, and providing more voice leading possibilities—it normally requires the purchase of additional strings and the labor of installation on each student's instrument.

Style

Aesthetically, there is no particular style that is best for students as long as the instrument is of a traditional design (no flying-V ukuleles!); however, if the school is providing instruments, it is worth considering the maturity level of students before committing to working with an assortment of styles. For some students, the preoccupation over having or not having a particular style can present an unnecessary distraction from making music. In any case, teachers may take the opportunity to illustrate that the way an instrument looks often does not correlate with the quality of the sound.

Tuning Mechanisms

The simple machine of the geared tuner requires a less sensitive touch from the user than friction peg tuners (which turn the string at a 1:1 ratio), so students typically find geared tuners easier to use when they begin tuning their own instruments.

Protection

Any school instruments that students will take home should be protected with foamboard or hard-shell cases. These should be purchased at the same time as the ukuleles, if the school is making the purchase. For instruments remaining in the school, a padded gig bag will suffice. Unpadded gig bags basically only protect the instrument from getting wet and are barely worthwhile. The cardboard box that the instrument comes in will generally not survive the year as a method of in-school storage, especially if the instrument is constantly being taken out and put away.

II

UP AND RUNNING

4

CLASSROOM MANAGEMENT

Adding ukuleles to a classroom environment requires organization and forethought as to how, where, and when the instruments will be handled and played. As with most classroom management issues, addressing them once they have become problematic is often too late. This section offers tips specific to the ukulele classroom that can help ensure a maximally productive and enjoyable experience from the start.

SETTING UP THE ROOM

As in any classroom, the arrangement of the physical space should reflect how the teacher would like the classmates to interact with each other and the teacher.

Seating Configurations

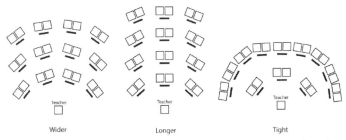

Wider   Longer   Tight

Figure 4.1.   Seating configurations showing students sitting in pairs, with music stands, oriented toward a common point, with space for the teacher to get physically near each student.

Use Chairs and Music Stands

Unless there are no chairs and/or music stands available, students should learn to play the ukulele while sitting in a chair and looking at any visual aids or sheet music on a music stand in front of them. Sitting on the floor, as is often done in some elementary music classes, will make it difficult to use good posture, and not using music stands will require students to divert their eyes away from the teacher more frequently.

Orient Chairs to the Teacher's Line of Sight

This can be done by literally standing behind each seat and turning it in the direction you would like the student to be focused. Ideally, students should be able to look straight ahead and make eye contact with the teacher in a manner similar to band or orchestral seating (fig. 4.1). Avoid circular seating or arrangements in which some students are always seeing the teacher's side or back.

Seat Students in Pairs

Seating students in pairs, with a walkable space around them, ensures that the teacher can get physically next to each student in the room (fig. 4.1). If any students are seated in an area that the teacher cannot reach easily, it will be difficult to help them individually when necessary. Being able to easily circulate the room is also an effective way for the teacher to deter off-task behavior.

Raise Music Stands to Eye Level

Again, to make it easier to maintain eye contact, it helps for any visual references on the music stand to be as close as possible to the student's direct line of sight. Raising the music stand a bit higher than normal makes it easier for students to glance back and forth from the music stand to the teacher.

USING SHARED INSTRUMENTS

If home use of the instruments is not possible, the retrieval and return of classroom instruments must be efficient and organized.

Have Students Use the Same Instrument Each Class

This can be done by simply numbering each instrument (with an indelible marker on the back of the headstock and on cases) and assigning a number to each student in each class. While it is possible to use ukuleles interchangeably (no sanitizing necessary), using the same instrument each time gives students a greater sense of ownership of, and respect for, the instrument. It also makes it easier for the teacher to hold students accountable for any misuse or damage and generally contributes to a more orderly classroom.

Minimize Obstacles to Retrieving Instruments

If space allows, it is best to install u-shaped brackets (a few dollars each) from which the ukuleles can hang openly along the wall. This eliminates the need for packing and unpacking them into cases and thus conserves instructional time. It also makes it easier to tune instruments faster. If the instruments cannot be stored this way, an organized shelving system in the room is sufficient for storing instruments in cases. The number of each instrument should be clearly displayed in any storage system, such that instruments are returned to the same place each time.

Have a Case for Each Instrument

Even if instruments can be hung on the wall, there may come a time when it is necessary to move or store them. The cardboard box in which new ukuleles are packaged is neither space-saving nor durable enough for long-term storage. Padded gig bags are a particularly inexpensive way to protect ukuleles from the elements, gravity, and wear and tear, and can also be compressed for storage when not in use.

TUNING INSTRUMENTS

Students should become independent tuners of their instrument as soon as possible, but beginners will need the teacher to tune the instrument at first. Bear in mind that the newer a ukulele is, the more frequently it will fall out of tune. New strings can take up to several weeks before they settle in.

Tune Instruments Before Class, If Time Allows

Instruments stored in the classroom can be tuned by the teacher during any available time, but instruments coming from home can also be brought to the classroom at the beginning of the school day for tuning. This will help conserve instructional time and simplify the classroom routine.

Practice Tuning If You Are Inexperienced

Whether tuning takes place during or outside class time, the teacher should be able to tune a student's ukulele in a matter of seconds. Practicing will exercise the teacher's ear and get her/him used to which direction each tuner twists for raising or lowering the pitch.

If Tuning during Class, Keep All Students Engaged

Students waiting to be tuned, or just having been tuned, will be idle unless they have a stake in the tuning of other students or have another task to accomplish in the meantime. Whether by making a game out of it, giving short reading or writing tasks, using a buddy system, or using students as tuning assistants (who are capable of self-tuning), all students should remain engaged.

Teach Students How to Use Tuning Forks

When students are ready to tune their own instrument, tuning forks are perhaps the least expensive, quietest, and most educational way to learn how to tune (see the method described in chapter 2). By touching the base of the tuning fork to the body of the ukulele, its sound becomes naturally amplified, and the a-string will visibly vibrate when perfectly in tune, even if not plucked—a great opportunity for a mini-lesson in acoustics!

LANGUAGE AND TERMINOLOGY

When verbally describing chords, notes, locations, or directional movements to a class, it is important for the teacher to keep the use of language and terminology precise and consistent in order to avoid confusion.

Use "Right" and "Left" When Giving Directions for Hand Positions on the Neck

Experienced string players may speak of playing "up the neck" and "down the neck," but this is confusing language for beginners because of the inverse relationship between pitch and hand position. As the hand moves to a lower position on the neck, the pitch goes up, and vice versa. Since the instrument is viewed horizontally while playing, "left" and "right" are more precise terms (or otherwise "toward the head" and "toward the sound hole").

Describe String Locations in Relation to the Player

When working with students who do not know the strings by name or number yet, descriptions like "the top string," "the bottom string," or "the next string up" can be confusing. From the player's perspective, strings at a lower altitude visually appear above strings that are at a higher altitude. Saying "the string closest to the floor" or "the next string closer to your chin," for example makes it clearer.

Differentiate Between "Frets" and "Fret Wires"

Technically speaking, the raised metal bands going across the neck of the ukulele are fret *wires*, though they are commonly just called "frets." But when teaching students about frets as a guide to where their fingers belong, it is helpful to define a fret as a "box" or the "space between the lines." If "fret" and "fret wire" are used synonymously, it becomes unclear exactly where the finger belongs. (Does saying "third fret" mean that the finger goes above the third line? Below it? On the line itself?)

Use Full Names for Major Chords

Experienced musicians commonly refer to major chords by their letter name only (that is, "C" instead of "C major"), but if the teacher uses this language it may be unclear to students whether s/he is talking about a note or a chord. Although chord charts commonly abbreviate the names of major chords in this manner as well, the teacher should similarly use the full name of the chord in any printed materials for beginners.

Use Lowercase Letters for Note Names

As is done in this book, printed materials should use lowercase letters for note names in order to distinguish them from chord names. In typed materials, using "flat" and "sharp" instead of using "b" and "#" (which are not music font symbols) is also clearer.

MANAGING STUDENT BEHAVIOR

While the ukulele is virtually incapable of obnoxious sounds and does not easily lend itself to use as an imaginary weapon, it is still important to maintain a code of conduct.

Enforce a Zero-Tolerance Policy for Playing at Improper Times

Students who play their instrument at improper times—no matter how quietly or briefly—are not paying attention and may be distracting other students. Having students put the instrument away for a few minutes (or having the teacher take it away) is an effective form of conditioning that both quiets the room quickly and modifies future behavior for most students.

Teach "Resting" and "Ready" Positions

It helps for students to have a distinct "resting" position to use when not playing, for which the teacher may call on occasion. Identifying the position used for playing as "playing position" may cause some students to think it is appropriate to play once they are in the position. "Ready" is more precise.

Discourage Self-Tuning Before It Has Been Taught

After only a few lessons, many students will begin to know when their instrument "doesn't sound right" without any help. This in itself should be praised, as it represents good aural perception and is the first step in being able to tune the instrument. But until students are taught how to tune independently, the proper response should be for them to inform the teacher that their instrument is out of tune rather than adjust the tuners on their own.

STRUCTURING CLASS TIME

The goal of any experience with the ukulele should be for students to do as much playing as possible. Teacher instructions should be simple and direct, and transitions should be quick and smooth.

Include a Warm-Up

If instruments have been tuned before class, students can join a warm-up as soon as they arrive and get set up. Even if tuning has to be done in class, a warm-up helps the group focus together and is a good opportunity to review or prepare for new material.

Keep the Beat Going

To avoid "down time" that can lead to off-task behavior, the teacher may create musical continuity between exercises and songs by continuing the beat (through snapping, stomping, using a loud metronome or electronic drum beat, etc.) after students are finished playing. Give new directions over the beat (or *to* the beat) as necessary—including to repeat passages that may not have been performed satisfactorily—but do not stop the flow unless absolutely necessary.

Keep Everyone Singing

Being able to sing and play is one of the best attributes of the ukulele, and singing should comprise a substantial part of any lesson. The act of playing the ukulele while reading the notes and singing them does take practice to execute well, and students will adjust at different rates. In general the teacher should not let the ukulele become an obstacle to singing but rather make it a reward for it. In cases where students have stopped singing to concentrate more on their ukulele playing, the teacher should have them stop playing until they can comfortably sing the part, then try the part with the ukulele.

Use Varied Repetition

Students need many attempts to practice when learning any task, and some-times the school will be the only place they can play the ukulele. There are a variety of ways to vary the repetition of any exercise, scale, excerpt, or complete piece of music to keep it from becoming monotonous, including:

1. Changing the pitch, rhythm, tempo, volume, or duration
2. Changing the sequence
3. Having student(s) lead or solo
4. Splitting the class into groups with different roles
5. Changing the groups/Switching group roles
6. Creating a narrative or game as a framework

The more spontaneously variation is introduced, the more engaging the lesson is likely to be.

PROMOTING HOME PRACTICE

Though the ukulele may be easier for beginners than many other instruments, students must still develop discipline and understand that they cannot improve their playing without it.

Involve Parents

Meet with parents or send a letter home before even beginning the program, explaining expectations for student preparedness, instrument care, and concrete ways to support learning at home. Then, follow up periodically especially with parents of students who are falling behind or excelling beyond expectations.

Distribute Printed Materials

Students should have song sheets, diagrams, and general reference materials to support them (and to help involved parents give support at home) in their home practice. A three-ring binder is a good way for students to store sheet music and class handouts. Loose papers, even if kept in a folder, tend to get lost.

Use an Assignment Sheet/Practice Log

Each student should know precisely what their assignment is each week and where to find it. Students should write their assignments down themselves and have their practice certified with parental initials.

Make It Easy for Students to Track Their Progress

Using a reward system, creating "levels" to achieve, or otherwise setting clear goals for students and keeping track of them can help students experience more positive reinforcement as a result of home practice.

MAINTENANCE AND REPAIRS

Most students implicitly realize that the ukulele is not as durable as, say, a plastic recorder, and tend to treat it with greater respect as a result. Even in cases where the instrument suffers abuse or accidents, well-made ukuleles are surprisingly resilient. Still the occasional repair may be necessary.

Replacing Strings

Strings come separately packaged and labeled according to the pitch they are to hold (they are *not* interchangeable). When re-stringing, bear in mind that it is common to have to re-tune new strings frequently for up to several weeks before they hold their pitch with consistency.

All ukuleles use the same system for threading strings through the tuners and wrapping around them, which involves rotating the tuners *outward* to tighten the strings (fig. 4.2). Once the string is tuned, excess string should be snipped as closely as possible.

Threading through the bridge can differ depending on the make of the instrument. Some lower quality ukuleles use a system in which one end of the string is tied in a simple knot and slipped through a notch. A more secure system, found on better quality ukuleles, involves threading the string through a hole in the bridge and wrapping it around itself (fig. 4.3).

Re-Stringing the Ukulele Head

Figure 4.2. To tighten the strings the tuning peg turns outward.

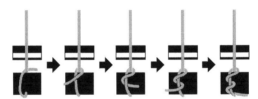

Figure 4.3. Sequence for fastening strings to the bridge.

Excess string may be closely snipped at both ends once the string is tightened into place. It takes a lot to snap a ukulele string in two. Only after long periods of regular usage may they become worn on the underside by the fretwires. Otherwise, the bridge is more likely to rip off before the string breaks from any unwarranted and excessive over-tightening.

Tightening the Tuners

Whether the tuners are wooden pegs or metal gears, both can become loose and cause the instrument to slip out of tune easily. In both cases, the solution is simply to tighten the screw located on the back of the spindle around which the strings are wound. (In the case of tuning pegs, the spindle is the peg itself and the screw is in the middle of the knob.)

Fixing Buzzing Notes

If there is a buzzing sound when any of the open strings are played, check to make sure none of the strings have fallen out of alignment in the nut and that there are no loose objects (including excess uncut string) in or on the instrument. If only certain fretted notes buzz, the problem may be that the next fret wire toward the sound hole may be too high. Frets can be sanded or filed down, but as this is a permanent modification to the instrument it should be done with caution or otherwise taken to a professional.

Replacing a Snapped Bridge

When the bridge is such that it is glued on to the body of the ukulele, it is vulnerable to snapping off (on cheaply made ukuleles, this may happen without provocation). On expensive models, the reattachment should be done by a luthier, but for a student ukulele it is not worth the expense. Upon detaching the strings from the bridge and removing dried glue, *wood glue* can be used to affix the bridge to its original location (as precisely as possible) and a clamp or otherwise a heavy object can be used to hold it in place while it dries. The instrument should not be restrung then for at least 48 hours.

5

INTRODUCING STUDENTS TO THE UKULELE

The first day with instruments is exciting for everyone involved and provides opportunities for the teacher to set the tone for future lessons, not unlike the first day of school. To better plan and implement a ukulele program, it is best to introduce the instrument after more general classroom routines and expectations have been firmly established and the teacher has developed some individualized knowledge of students.

ACCOMMODATING (SPECIAL) LEARNERS

Many practices for accommodating special learners also make for good teaching that will maximize the clarity and effectiveness of lessons for all students.

Pre-Teaching and Modeling

The first day with instruments should be focused on playing and singing with the ukulele. As such it is best for the teacher to spend time in *prior* lessons teaching vocabulary, modeling proper care and classroom procedures with the instrument, reviewing conducting cues, and covering any other related material that does necessitate students having the instrument in their hands. By the time students take the instrument out in the classroom, they should already know:

1. Where to find their ukulele and when to retrieve it (if stored in the music room).
2. When, where, and how cases should be opened and stored.
3. What to do with the ukulele once it is out of the case.
4. How to handle the ukulele with care.
5. The name and location of the major parts (head, neck, body).
6. When to begin playing and when to stop.

For the first few lessons, depending on the age of the students, the teacher may wish to have everyone perform the same tasks involving handling the instrument at the same time. One effective way to test for understanding of proper conduct with the ukulele is for the teacher to switch roles with students, demonstrate the *incorrect* behavior, and have the students correct him/her.

Modifying the Instrument

No permanent modifications should be made to a student's ukulele, but small adhesive labels may help in orienting students to the instrument. Since beginners tend to do most of their playing in the first four frets, the fret marker on the fifth fret does not function well as a reference point. Small color-coding dot labels may be placed under the strings where the fingers should be pressed for certain chords or notes (fig. 5.1).

Each color may correspond to a different chord, but it is best to limit the number of markers to three. Likewise, the open strings may be labeled below the bridge or to the *right* of each string above the sound hole (when the instrument is held in playing position the label will appear as if it is directly under the string) (fig. 5.2). The teacher should use discretion in how long such labels remain on the instrument to avoid unnecessary dependence on them.

Figure 5.1. Color-coding dots used as chord position markers.

Figure 5.2. The open strings, labeled

Using Alternate Notation

Ukulele chord diagrams represent the frets and strings of the ukulele as they would appear if one were looking directly at the ukulele; however, since this does not conform to how the ukulele looks from the player's perspective while playing, some students may have trouble translating the chord diagram into practice. To help them, the teacher may use diagrams that are rotated 90 degrees to the left, so that the lines representing the frets are vertical and the lines representing the strings are horizontal—just as they appear on the instrument to the student (fig. 5.3).

Using chord diagrams that show finger numberings is also critical for students to learn the proper position for new chords (chord diagrams appearing in commercial sheet music typically do not show fingering). See the appendix for standard and rotated diagrams of common chords with fingerings.

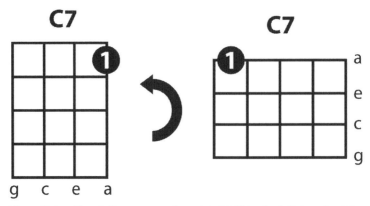

Figure 5.3. Chord diagrams can be rotated 90° to the left to reflect the way the player views the strings and frets while playing.

Drilling and Repetition

In music, the "drill" doesn't have to "kill." Rather, it can be a useful way to develop the basis for *skill*. Students need some of their knowledge to become "automatic" in order to become fluent in locating notes and chords on the instrument, including:

- *The Names of the Open Strings*—A mnemonic device such as "Good Cooks Eat A lot" (or anything better students can come up with) is an essential memory trick for beginners. One practice that can be used as a regular warm-up activity for introductory classes is to have students cycle through each of the open strings in a repeating rhythm with light accompaniment from the teacher on a bass or piano. This type of exercise is open to much variation but might look something like figures 5.4a–b.

  The teacher can begin calling out strings in a random order to test for understanding (harmonic accompaniment for this does not have to conform to proper voice leading or traditional chord resolutions—a major triad in root position for each note is fine—the point is to provide "backup" and help the exercise sound musical and dynamic).

- *Left Hand Finger Numbering*—To quickly drill a class on finger numbering, have them hold up all five fingers of their left hand and touch the fingers to their thumb as the teacher calls out individual numbers and combinations. This reinforces the type of hand position they will

Open String Exercise

Figure 5.4a. An example of a warm-up using the open strings with accompaniment by the teacher.

Figure 5.4b.

use when actually fretting chords with these fingers. *Do not* drill fingering by asking students to hold up each finger one at a time. While it works fine for fingers 1, 3, and 4, the teacher will receive an offensive gesture from the entire class when identifying finger 2!

- *Fret Numbering*—To quickly drill students on fret numbers, have them hold their ukulele upright and facing the teacher. Ask them to lay their pointer finger across fret 1, touching all four strings, then try frets 2, 3, and 4, then skip around. The teacher may model along with the class, then have them do it on their own. To test for understanding they may count the total number of frets on the ukulele.

While drills should not comprise more than a few minutes of a class period, they do not need to be dry and boring. See chapter 4: "Use Varied Repetition" for ways of keeping drill activities interesting.

Teaching How to Practice

Most students are familiar with the idea of practicing but many may be unclear about what it actually looks like. It is worthwhile to spend time deriving the meaning of effective practice with students, especially if they can take their instruments home. Boiling it down to a few staples—such as playing slowly, working on short sections and then connecting them, and aiming for a high ratio of correct executions to incorrect—can make it more easily digestible. Any such definition of practice can be translated into an enumerated procedure of concrete steps to follow, given to all students and parents in hard copy form. This can even begin with such banalities as finding a quiet place, getting a chair, and setting up sheet music. The teacher can also ask students to come up with a reasonable schedule for this regimen that they can actually stick to, and have this schedule signed by parents at the beginning of the year. Then, students can indicate each week whether they stuck to the schedule and, if not, revise it as needed.

Giving Clear Assignments

All assignments given by the teacher should be put in writing, either by the teacher or student, and be supported with printed or otherwise visually accessible reference materials or sheet music. A verbal instruction like "Practice changing between C and G7 for next week," while short and simple, will likely fall by the wayside as soon as students leave the room. Any materials given to students should also be printed rather than handwritten or hand-drawn where at all possible and should also demonstrate consistent use of language and terminology (see chapter 4).

OBJECTIVES OF THE VERY FIRST LESSON

Students should leave their first lesson with the ukulele being able to:

1. Demonstrate resting and ready positions.
2. Strum a chord with good technique.
3. Pluck string(s) with good technique.
4. Sing a familiar song while playing.
5. Store the instrument properly.
6. Go home knowing what to practice (take-home instruments only).

Figure 5.5. The "resting" position

Positions

Teaching how to hold the instrument includes two positions: the playing position and the "resting" position. In resting position, the instrument simply lies across their lap (fig. 5.5).

Whether students are left- or right-handed, the head of the instrument should always be on their left (for young students who have not mastered left from right, use a feature of each side of the room, such as "door" or "window").

The younger students are, the more these two positions will need to be explicitly differentiated and drilled. The teacher may wish to call the playing position "ready position" so students understand they may not always be making sound in that position.

Strumming

The downward strum with the thumb is the least complicated and most intuitive strum for most people learning to play the ukulele. Since the open strings generate a consonant chord (C6 in root position, or Am7 in first inversion), students do not need any left-hand technique to play their first real chord. Students may practice strumming by performing various rhythms on the open chord, either from notation or by rote, and the teacher may accompany from another instrument.

Depending on their age and ability level, students may begin learning fretted chords in their first lesson as well. To teach fretted chords, students should be versed in ukulele fingering. Unlike the piano, ukulele fingering begins at the index finger, which is the finger people commonly hold up when they represent counting as a hand gesture. It is important to teach the position of the entire hand for each chord, including the thumb, no matter how many fingers are actually used on the fretboard. Simply reminding students of the thumb's position on the back of the neck alone will help orient their hand to the correct position for most beginning chords. Unused fingers should not be curled away, or sticking straight up, but rather floating above the fretboard in a relaxed manner.

Picking

Using the thumb in downward motion is the simplest technique for beginners to use in plucking strings. Though strumming may be done with other fingers, the thumb will always be required in plucking any melody at any level. The forearm should remain anchored on the body of the ukulele and the only movement should come from the wrist, with the thumb finishing the motion not far from where it started.

Singing and Playing a Song

Students should go home knowing how to sing and play *something* on the ukulele after their first day. At the very least, any so-mi/so-mi-la song or simple round can be performed over a C major chord strummed to the beat. Older groups may be able to play songs with two or three chords in the first lesson. In any case, the song should be one with which students are already familiar with the tune and words. For a list of songs by chords, see the appendix.

Storing the Instrument

If instruments are in cases, students may be tempted to open them on their lap or even in mid-air because they are so small and light. Rather, cases should be both opened and closed on the floor to prevent being dropped accidentally. Instruments should also never be put in cases without the case immediately being fastened shut. During class, cases should be kept under the seats or otherwise in a storage area, but never in the aisles and rows.

Homework Assignment (Take-Home Instruments Only)

Students should immediately get in the habit of going home to practice what they have learned. Use of an assignment sheet/practice log, and also printed reference materials, should begin with the very first lesson. Parents should be made aware of home practice expectations, and the practice log should include an area for them to initial in acknowledgment of each assignment.

6

TECHNICAL SEQUENCE

As the technical goals for students will differ depending on their age, abilities, the setting, frequency of meetings, and whether students have their own instruments, this section suggests a general sequence for the technique of both hands to bear in mind while choosing literature, planning lessons, arranging music, or setting goals for individual classes or groups. Beginner groups can perform fine with even the most basic techniques, with many of the more advanced techniques being more characteristic of solo instrumental playing.

STRUMMING AND PICKING

Techniques for strumming and picking include:

1. Downward Strum: Thumb
2. Picking: Thumb
3. Downward Strum: Index Finger
4. Upward Strum: Index Finger
5. Strumming Patterns: Index Finger
6. Picking: Multiple Fingers
7. Palm-Muting
8. Upward Strum: Thumb
9. Ornamental Strums

Note that techniques involving a soft felt pick or the use of a fingernail for picking are not included here. Additional strumming techniques that involve work from both hands in conjunction are described in the "Fretting and Related Techniques" section.

Downward Strum: Thumb

This is a "soft" downward strum, using the fleshy part on the outward side of the thumb. Contact with the strings, as always, should happen where the neck meets the body of the ukulele. The hand should remain open, with the other fingers relaxed yet away from the strings and the body of the ukulele. See figure 2.6 in chapter 2 (p. 19).

Picking: Thumb

Using the same part of the thumb as for the downward strum, the thumb may pluck melodies on one or more strings. The thumb should not pull from under the strings and the hand should not fly away from the ukulele after making contact with each string. Rather, the movement should come from very slight pivoting from the wrist with the forearm firmly anchored on the body of the ukulele. This technique will carry students through playing many simple melodies.

Downward Strum: Index Finger

This is a "hard" downward strum, using the tip of the nail of the right index finger. The nail gives it a brighter sound than the downward strum using the thumb and is also more durable. Students should be careful not to curve their finger in too far inward, lest their cuticle become irritated from making contact with the strings. To support the index finger, the thumb may be placed between its middle two joints. The finger starts in a curved position where it is pointing toward the player, then with an outward flick of the wrist, the finger makes contact with all of the strings and ends extended, pointing straight at the floor (see figure 2.7 [p. 20] in chapter 2).

Students should move to this strum from thumb strumming as soon as they are comfortable with holding the instrument, identifying the open strings, and fretting basic chords like C and F.

Upward Strum: Index Finger

Using the same hand position as the downward strum, the fleshy part of the index finger may make contact with the strings on the way back *up* after any downward motion of the hand. The upward strum will naturally be softer and generally falls on upbeats. Not normally used in isolation, this technique is best practiced by adding it between beats of the regular downward strum. By strumming between the beats, this pattern creates more fluidity than a simple downward strum on each beat. It may be performed straight or with a swing.

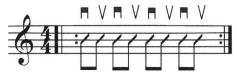

Figure 6.1a. Strumming pattern including up-strums

Strumming Patterns: Index Finger

The fingers may avoid contact with the strings at certain points in the hand's recurring down-up motion to produce different strum patterns. These may be illustrated with rhythm notation (indicating when to strum) accompanied by strum notation (indicating which direction the hand is moving). Even if the rhythm is syncopated or contains empty beats, the hand typically continues to move to the beat. Thus, downstrums will happen on downbeats and upstrums will happen on upbeats. Some common strum patterns include:

Picking: Multiple Fingers

To play faster melodic passages or those that include arpeggios or broken chords in which more than one note is played at once, it is necessary to use more than one finger. While the thumb plucks away from the player, the other fingers pluck towards the player, using the fleshy part of the fingertip to pull the string slightly before releasing (nails should only be used if grown out for this purpose). The hand itself should maintain a steady position with the thumb and fingers all above the strings, ready to play. Fingers may be indicated in tablature using classical guitar abbreviations for the finger names (*p*: Thumb, *i*: Index, *m*: Middle, *a*: Ring, *c*: Pinky) (fig. 6.1c).

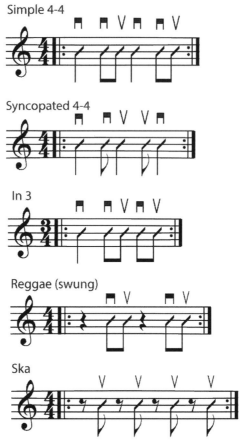

Figure 6.1b.   Common strumming patterns

Figure 6.1c.   Example of fingerpicking notated with classical guitar fingering symbols.

Palm-Muting

Any note or chord can be muted by leaning the pinky-side of the palm on all of the strings near the bridge of the ukulele while strumming or plucking the strings. This can be indicated in tablature using "P.M." with a dashed line to indicate the duration of the mute (fig. 6.2). The palm can also be used to shorten the sustain on notes that have already been strummed (damping).

Figure 6.2.   Palm-mute notation

Upward Strum: Thumb

The tip of the nail of the thumb can be used to produce a "hard" strum on the way up following any downward motion of the hand in order to accent weak beats or off beats. Not normally used in isolation, this technique is best practiced in strumming patterns that feature accented upbeats. Note that the thumb must pass below all of the strings on the way down so it may make contact on the way up.

Ornamental Strums

Some strums are used for momentary embellishment rather than as a sustained pattern. These often involve quick, gestural movements, in which multiple fingers make contact with the strings on the way down and/or up. They take considerably more practice than other strums but are very effective in adding a bit of flair to otherwise commonplace patterns.

Some common strums of this variety include:

- *The Double Strum*—This ornament normally precedes a strong beat or downbeat. It combines an upstrum with the thumb (nail) followed by an upstrum with the index finger in quick succession. It is typically completed by a regular downward strum with the index finger on the next beat.

Figure 6.3. Double-strum

- *The Triple Strum*—The triple strum consists of a downward strum with the index finger followed by an upward strum with the thumb and an upward strum with the index finger, all in a triplet rhythm. It is important that the thumb pass beyond the strings on the initial index finger strum so that it is in a position to make contact with the strings on the way up. Unlike the double strum, this ornament may be repeated several times in succession.

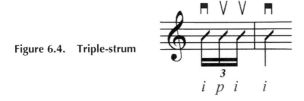

Figure 6.4. Triple-strum

- *The Fan Strum*—The fan strum is a way to embellish a downbeat or strong beat itself. It begins slightly before the beat but, as a downward strum, continues through it. In the fan strum, each fingertip begins pointed toward the player and makes contact with the strings in very quick succession from the pinky to the index finger, ending with all fingers extended.

Figure 6.5. Fan strum

FRETTING AND RELATED TECHNIQUES

Hand position is at least as important as proper fingering for the fretting hand as both affect the ability to execute and easily transition between chords. It is critical for students to use the correct fingering consistently for both chords and scales to keep their playing simple and smooth. Often the same basic hand shape can be used for different chords, even those that do not involve all four strings.

Fretting and related techniques include:

1. Fretted Notes and One-Finger Chords
2. Two-Finger Chords
3. Three-Finger Chords
4. One- and Two-Finger Barre Chords
5. Three-Finger Barre and Four-Finger Chords
6. Muting
7. Sliding
8. Scrubbing
9. Hammering On
10. Pulling Off

Fretted Notes and One-Finger Chords

Learning to fret a note using one finger at a time allows a student to play melodies and scales as well as seven different chords. It is best to begin on the first string (**a**), as there is less risk of the finger muting other strings by touching them. Since the ukulele is very friendly to songs and melodies in the key of C, learning to play the C major chord is an ideal place to start. It allows students to accompany themselves singing any so-mi/so-mi-la song or one-chord song/round. From C7—easy to locate in the first fret, on the first string, with the first finger—students can move a single finger to neighboring frets and strings to learn up to six other chords (not necessarily usable together in one song), beginning with Cmaj7 and C major (fig. 6.6).

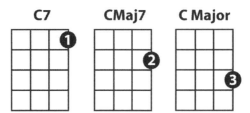

Figure 6.6. C7, Cmaj7, and Cmajor are good
starting chords for beginners.

Reaching over open strings, students can also play four additional chords fretting only one string at a time.

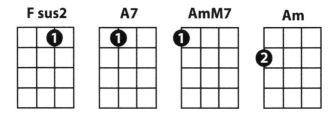

Fsus4 is functional as a regular F major chord in many songs. AmMaj7 is more of a jazz chord but also may be used as a passing chord between A minor and Amin7.

Two-Finger Chords

Fretting two strings requires two fingers to apply the appropriate force in fretting, with one or both reaching over open strings. Working from the A-minor chord formation, adding the third finger yields a D7 chord. This same formation can be relocated or slightly modified to produce several other useful chords.

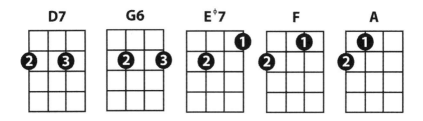

Three-Finger Chords

Chords that use three fingers on three different frets are easiest initially, as they are the most "roomy" formations.

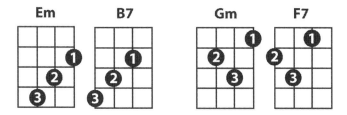

Other three-finger chords involve fretting parallel strings in the same fret with different fingers—requiring the hand to turn a bit outward to avoid "crowded" fingers. Some of these chords use the same formation as two-finger chords described above, only with an added finger.

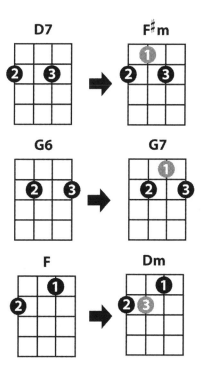

Other three-finger chords require new formations:

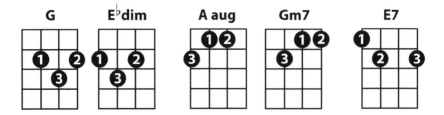

One- and Two-Finger Barre Chords

A single finger can also be used across all four strings in the same fret to produce chord formations at higher pitches on the neck. These can be called *barre chords*, as with guitar. In some cases, the middle finger may "piggy-back" on top of the index finger in order to provide extra force in pressing all four of the strings down. In cases where the fourth string is fretted by a different finger, it is not necessary to barre across all four strings, only the first three. Up to two fingers can produce formations for major, minor, suspended fourth, sixth (relative minor seventh), seventh, and major seventh chords that can be transposed to any key.

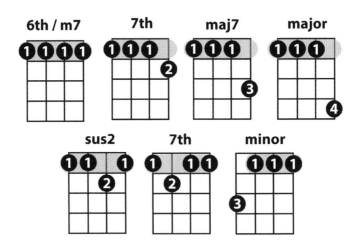

Three-Finger Barre and Four-Finger Chords

Chords that use one finger on each string may be among the more technically demanding but also offer the greatest amount of control. Any single note in the chord may be sustained or dampened at any time, making it easier to execute *legato* or *staccato* effects in pieces that combine melodic and harmonic elements. In many cases, a barre can be used to make the chord formation more comfortable and easier for switching to other chords.

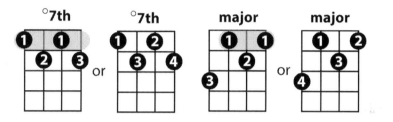

Muting

Muting with the fretting hand simply involves touching all of the strings—but not pressing them down—while strumming in order to prevent them from ringing. While muting is not technically difficult in isolation, the ability to mix it into a regular strum pattern requires greater control and coordination. If done *before* the chord has been strummed, it will create an unpitched "chnk" sound rather than an identifiable chord (in some circles referred to as the "Z" or "Zed" chord). In rhythmic notation, this type of chord may be indicated with an "x" notehead (fig. 6.14). If done *after* a chord has been strummed, it will shorten the duration of the chord by deadening the vibration of the strings.

Bo Diddley Beat (Clave Rhythm)

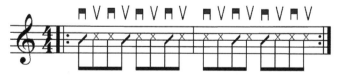

Figure 6.14. Strumming pattern with muted strums

Sliding

Sliding allows the player to slur from one note to another note on the same string with the same finger. A fretted string is plucked while the finger fretting the string slides to a different fret while maintaining pressure on the string. If the finger passes through many frets in one sweeping motion, it will create a *glissando* effect. This technique can also be extended to use with chord formations, especially those that involve fretting on all four strings.

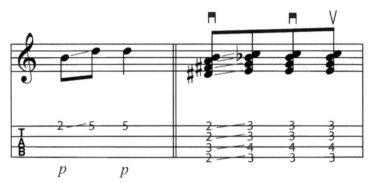

Figure 6.15. Slides, notated with diagonal lines in tablature and treble staff notation.

Scrubbing

Upon mastering any chord formation that involves fretting all four strings, it is possible to "scrub" the chord by temporarily sliding the formation to, from, or back and forth between neighboring frets while strumming. This use of neighboring tones can add style to otherwise static harmony or can be used for a cadential effect.

Figure 6.16. "Scrubbing" a C7 chord.

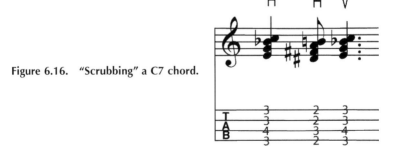

Hammering On

One way to slur notes on the ukulele is to pluck an open or fretted string and slam down a finger from the fretting hand onto a fret yielding a higher pitch. The percussive force used by the finger on the string (like a hammer) makes the string ring without being plucked again. Note that this technique can only be used going from a lower pitch to a higher one.

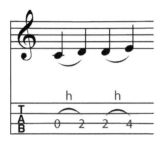

Figure 6.17. Using a "hammer-on" technique to slur between ascending notes.

Pulling Off

Another way to slur notes on the ukulele is to pluck a fretted note and have a finger from the fretting hand grab slightly under the string before releasing it from the fret. If there is another finger fretting the string at a lower pitch, that pitch will ring, otherwise the open string will ring. Note that this technique can only be used going from a higher pitch to a lower one.

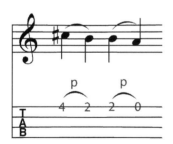

Figure 6.18. Using "pull-off" technique to slur between descending notes.

7

APPLICATIONS IN
CLASSROOM MUSIC

When using the ukulele as a classroom instrument, the focus is more on developing music literacy than virtuoso ukulele performers. The ukulele offers the advantage of being able to isolate (or combine) the elements of rhythm, melody, and harmony, with a low threshold of technical skill required to do so. In this setting, mastery of the ukulele itself should be thought of as a collateral long-term effect of using it as a hands-on tool in learning transferrable knowledge and skills.

This chapter offers ways students can use the ukulele in learning about music theory and notation, improvising, composing, and ear training. For maximum effectiveness, chapters 5 and 6 should be consulted before planning and setting up any classroom lessons with the ukulele.

READING RHYTHMS

Students can play rhythms on the ukulele with very little technical ability, making rhythm activities suitable for any learning level. At its most basic, students can strum a muted chord to perform any rhythm or even tap the body of the instrument with the thumb or fingertips. Use of these unpitched sounds effectively turns the ukulele into a percussion instrument (albeit much quieter!). Pitch may be introduced as a means of varying repetition or as an opportunity for individual improvisation.

Example: To give students practice identifying the open strings by number or note name, the teacher may display a rhythmic pattern to be repeated; students may play rhythmic patterns on any of the open strings in unison as the teacher calls out changes to different strings at his/her discretion. As students learn fretted notes they may be added to this type of exercise.

Variation: Changing the patterns; playing in different groups; taking turns or playing in harmony.

Modified: Strum the C6 chord (no fretting or muting).

READING TREBLE STAFF PITCHES

Although mnemonic devices are useful (for example, "Every Good Boy Does Fine"), simply being able to translate music notation into letters is meaningless without the ability to create the corresponding sounds on an instrument or vocally. Introducing new treble staff notes as students learn how to play them gives students time to become familiar with how they look, sound, and feel—both in playing and singing—until they eventually become fluent readers of the treble clef.

Example: Using flash cards of the open string pitches, students may play quarter notes on the beat for whichever note the teacher displays. The teacher may reveal the name on the back of the card when it seems most students have correctly played the note, then move on to the next card in random order.

Variation: Add flash cards of fretted notes that students have learned. Use a repeating rhythmic pattern instead of playing on the beat, and have a student change the flash cards while the teacher improvises an accompaniment.

Modified: Do the exercise free of rhythm or a beat, and have students repeat the note at their own speed for a group tremolo effect.

MATCHING PITCH WHILE SINGING

The open strings and lower range of the ukulele covers the *tessitura* of soprano and alto range voices, including children's voices. This allows students to match the pitches of their voice and the ukulele while playing scales and melodies. As students learn to play and read scales, they may also sing the *solfège* syllables along with each pitch as a way of building a tonal memory of their sounds. Scales should coincide with learning related melodies (preferably one that uses all the notes of the scale and also stays within the octave).

Example: Students practice singing the pitches of the C pentatonic scale in *solfège*, then try to play them on the ukulele (two half notes or four quarters for each scale degree) while singing them. Students practice singing the verse from Stephen Foster's "Oh Susanna" in C pentatonic, then add the melody on the ukulele.

Variation: One group sings while another plays, then switch; one group plays chords while another plays melody and both sing; teacher accompanies in different styles.

Modified: Allow students to use the open **g** instead of fretting on the second string; include a counter-melodic part using more open string notes.

ANALYZING HARMONY

While it is capable of playing many kinds of music, the ukulele is perhaps most at home strumming the chords for a song. Having students perform harmonic analysis on songs they play can help them become familiar with common patterns and chord functions. Being able to identify diatonic chords in numerical form not only helps in analysis but also in social or professional performance settings. In heterogeneous groups where not all instruments may be in concert pitch, referring to chords by the numbers helps everyone speak the same language. Popular music provides a particularly rich source of music for these purposes, with chords often being few and uncomplicated.

Example: Students are given a song in an unfamiliar key with unfamiliar chords. After analyzing the chords using roman numerals, they transpose the song to a more familiar key with familiar chords in order to perform it.

Variation: Different song and chords; perform in different style; transpose to specific key given by the teacher; work in groups with different songs and/or keys for each group.

Modified: Write roman numerals for song given in a familiar key; song with fewer chords.

RECOGNIZING INTERVALS, CHORDS, AND CHORD CHANGES BY EAR

Reading music is a valuable tool, but students can use the ukulele to develop better aural skills for learning and performing music when sheet music may not be available. They develop a vocabulary of diatonic chords as soon as they begin learning how to play them, and by analyzing the harmony of songs (see previous section) can become familiar with their common functions in chord progressions. Likewise, as they develop a vocabulary of notes through singing and playing melodic music, they can become familiar with the characteristic sound of different intervals. These skills can be put to use by challenging students to figure out music on their own with incomplete information through listening.

Example: The teacher gives a starting chord for a familiar song (using familiar chords), and students must figure out the remaining chords—and when they change—by ear.

Variation: Use different songs/chords; students work in groups; all chord names given by teacher upfront plus an extraneous chord; use melodies instead of chords.

Modified: Shorter song/excerpt, fewer chords; chord pattern only (no lyrics or melody); melodies using only open strings and given note names.

IMPROVISING

With the open strings producing a consonant chord and containing the majority of notes in the C pentatonic and A minor pentatonic scales, the ukulele is very user-friendly for improvisation. As such, students can begin with simple improvisation exercises in these tonal environments without much technical skill or understanding of music theory. As students learn chords and songs containing more than one chord, they can use the chord fingerings for the song as the basis for melodic improvisation. Finally, the understanding of key and ability to locate specific notes associated with playing scales and modes can allow students to approach more advanced improvisation.

Example: The blues scale is unique in that it can be used for soloing over an entire progression of chords (with stylistically acceptable dissonances). By learning A7, D7, and E7 students can learn the changes for a 12-bar blues pattern in A.

12-Bar Blues in A

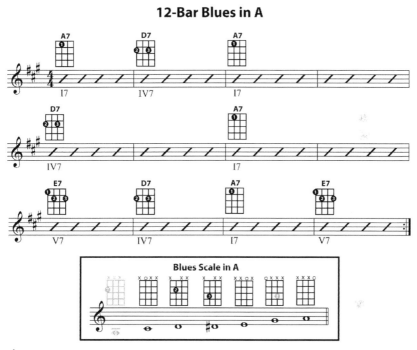

Figure 7.1.

The A minor pentatonic scale can be used as a kind of "gapped" blues scale in order to allow students to begin improvising over the pattern.

Variation: Change tempo, volume, style; solo verses alternate with group performance of chord progression; use the full blues scale for improvisation; use a different key; two students solo in dialogue with each other; solo using only notes from A7, D7, and E7 at the appropriate times.

Modified: Use only open strings for improvisation; play chords only on the changes; teacher provides accompaniment.

COMPOSING

As soon as students are familiar and comfortable with recognizing and playing even a small repertoire of notes, they may practice writing melodic music using what they know. As their musical vocabulary increases, the range, length, and complexity of compositions may increase. As long as compositions are kept within guidelines that will keep them technically playable by other students in the class, students can also exchange pieces and play each other's work.

Example: After reviewing how to draw all of the necessary symbols, students are given staff paper to compose an 8-bar melody in 4/4 time using only the notes of the C pentatonic scale and only quarter and half notes/rests. As they are writing, the teacher circulates to assist and play what they have written. Students then exchange papers and volunteer to play each other's compositions, with issues in notation clarity/accuracy highlighted by the teacher.

Variation: Change the scale, time signature, length, and/or rhythms used; add harmony; add chords; teacher improvises accompaniment of performed compositions.

Modified: Use only open strings, fewer different note/rest values; pre-print time signature, clef, and barlines on staff; use music notation software; compose as a class.

ILLUSTRATING ACOUSTIC PRINCIPLES AND MUSIC THEORY CONCEPTS

The physics of sound are perhaps more visible to students on stringed instruments than any other kind of instrument. Strings vibrate more visibly than do drumheads, bars, or air, and the means of changing pitch involves physically manipulating the instrument to shorten or lengthen the vibrating area of the string. This effectively illustrates the direct relationship between frequency and pitch, as well as the inverse mathematical relationship between frequency/pitch and string length (all other elements being constant).

Since Western music theory is very much based on the mathematical relationships between pitches, stringed instruments are also ideal for illustrating the concepts of half steps and whole steps, intervals, scales, and chords.

Frets, representing half-step intervals, appear more uniform than the keys of the piano keyboard or mallet percussion instruments. Soprano ukuleles are especially useful in that they have exactly twelve frets, with the twelfth fret being the octave of each open string and falling visibly at its midpoint. Students can see and feel that harmony involves at least two different tones sounding at the same time, and a chord involves at least three. They can also observe that a scale involves a series of pitches ascending to the octave (and descending back to the tonic), and that the octave can be divided into no more than twelve tones.

Example: Students use their knowledge of the major scale step pattern (w-w-h-w-w-w-h) to play a major scale starting on an open string and ending on the twelfth fret of the same string (place finger above the nut for scale degree 1). Students may also be challenged to identify the intervals that each of the fret markers indicates on the fretboard, relative to the pitch of the open string.

Variation: Change strings for different keys; use a different step pattern (different scale); students create their own step pattern; two groups play in canon to perform the scale in thirds (three groups for triads).

Modified: Do the exercise free of rhythm and allow students to tremolo on each note until each is playing the correct pitch; use chromatic scale.

INCORPORATING UKULELE INTO DALCROZE/ MUSIC-AND-MOVEMENT ACTIVITIES

Whereas the piano anchors the teacher in one location, the ukulele frees her/ him to circulate among students while accompanying music and movement activities. This allows the teacher to monitor certain students or even model certain types of movement during the activity. Strumming techniques, particularly those involving muted strums, also allow for a different variety of rhythmic accompaniment than is possible at the piano.

Example: Students pick a spot in the room and begin walking to the beat of a rhythmic pattern strummed by the teacher, who can also walk to the beat. When the teacher changes to a different chord, everyone must change direction. When the teacher performs a muted strum (no pitch) everyone walks in place.

Variation: Change the volume, tempo, or texture (switch to melodic playing); change the movement associated with changes in the music; include props such as scarves or ribbons.

Modified: Use a gymnasium or outdoor space for more room; use a pickup microphone and portable amplifier to enhance sound.

INCORPORATING UKULELE INTO ORFF SCHULWERK ACTIVITIES

Had the ukulele become popular in Europe much sooner than it did, Carl Orff and Gunild Keetman very well might have incorporated it into their "instrumentarium." The ukulele bears many of the characteristics of the instruments traditionally used in this approach, including its pleasant sound, simplicity, and relation to the pentatonic scale. The open strings of the ukulele can thus be used for playing the bi-tonic, tri-tonic, and tetra-tonic melodies that permeate the Orff repertoire and may also be used for improvisation in C pentatonic environments (fig. 7.2). If using low-fourth tuning, students can use the third and fourth string to play a bordun for C major or pentatonic melodies that do not go below c_4 (middle C).

Notes for Children's Melodies and Improvisation (Key of C)

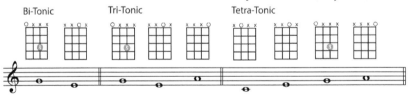

Figure 7.2.

Example: Using flash cards of two-beat rhythmic fragments, students work in groups to create longer rhythmic patterns. They first chant the pattern using the names of foods that fit each of the respective fragments, then perform the rhythm using body percussion. Finally, some of the students improvise a melody for the rhythm using the open strings of the ukulele while other students perform on pitched percussion instruments.

Variation: Use different, longer, or shorter rhythmic fragments; use different words for chanting (animals, sports teams, names, etc.); add unpitched percussion.

Modified: Strum the C6 chord (all open strings together) instead of plucking a melodic part.

8

UKULELES IN
PERFORMANCE

For ukulele clubs and ensembles, performance is a key aspect of the program, but classroom music students should participate in performances as well, given the learning opportunity it presents. The challenge and excitement of any kind of performance can be a powerful motivator and bring added focus to students in any program. Large semiannual concerts may be the prime example, but any occasion for students to show what they can do to anyone who has never seen or heard it counts as a performance. This can be as simple as inviting a teacher or other staff member into the room one day, or setting up a quick performance of one or two songs during a lunch period.

CHOOSING REPERTOIRE

Since the ukulele has a rather gentle learning curve, the teacher should initially choose repertoire that allows students to enjoy this rewarding aspect of the instrument. As stated in chapter 6, they should go home the very first day knowing how to sing and play a song, even if it only has one chord. While all learning processes have ceilings to break through at different times, helping students prolong the initial "honeymoon" phase with their new instruments can help engender more resilience later on. By reaching many achievable goals initially, they will have more belief in themselves when challenges inevitably come.

Though classroom programs may use the instrument in helping students learn music theory, students should by no means be restricted to performing only the music that they can understand on paper. The C major 7th chord is much easier to play than to understand. Likewise, many of the syncopated and inflected melodies in popular music are much easier to sing by ear than to read. It is like learning any other language: we would never try to tell toddlers they can only speak the words they know how to read. Rather, through speaking the words and learning how to use them, they come to recognize the symbols we use to represent them.

There is a growing body of music arranged explicitly for ukulele ensembles that is already of diverse genres, though it tends to be instrumental in nature and based more on melodic playing than strumming. This requires students to have a thorough knowledge of fingering and music notation but provides the opportunity for differentiated instruction (one of the parts is usually simpler or less technically demanding). The typical format includes at least two different parts written in standard notation, with each student's sheet music including all parts like a vocal score. The chord names, and sometimes chord diagrams, appear above the staff for reference, but the homogeneous instrumentation of a ukulele ensemble makes it difficult to hear melodic playing if too many other students are strumming chords (in the same range). This type of music can make for compelling performances and can also make it easier for the group to execute more complex harmonies and harmonic changes than when strumming chords.

Whereas more formal ukulele ensemble literature may not include singing or strumming, a less formal kind consists entirely of singing and strumming. Virtually any lead sheet for an individual ukulele player—consisting of the vocal part written on the treble staff with ukulele chord diagrams above—can be performed in unison by an entire group. Students having difficulty with chord fingering or changes may strum a more spare pattern (with more rests) to allow more time in changing positions. This type of "sing and strum" performance relies less on being able to read music and more on the ear. It is also more similar in nature to that of community ukulele ensembles found outside schools. Since it is possible to sing and play a song knowing only one chord, beginning students can rack up a collection of songs relatively fast. See the appendix for a list of songs for beginners using two chords or less.

Ideally, ukulele ensemble repertoire should demonstrate both the melodic and harmonic/rhythmic capabilities of the instrument, as well as the ability to sing and play at the same time. Working with more than one style of music—and notation—also helps prepare students for different musical opportunities in the future. Being able to read treble staff notation is useful for its precision and as a transferrable skill that a student can take to any other instrument, but following a chord chart, improvising, and being able to call out chords by the numbers is likewise a practical skill for rhythm section musicians in jazz and popular settings. No matter the style of notation, the repertoire should give students the tools as well as the desire to learn more.

ARRANGING MUSIC

Teacher-created arrangements allow for the tailoring of repertoire to the individual strengths, weaknesses, and tastes of the group. Since the range in student needs and abilities may vary widely, the teacher may create more challenging parts for advanced students while creating modified parts for slower-moving students that include more open strings, fewer different pitches, and/or simpler rhythms. This is a great way to keep all students participating in an ensemble of mixed abilities, ages, or amounts of experience.

Having only one type of instrument to worry about makes it fairly simple to arrange or even compose music for a ukulele ensemble. The ukulele is a non-transposing instrument and has a range that does not extend much above or below the treble staff. Vocal music that stays within the range of the ukulele can technically be performed on it with no adaptation necessary (longer note values may decay prematurely). Likewise, any music containing chord names can be performed on the ukulele simply by referring to ukulele chord diagrams. See the appendix for commonly used chord diagrams.

When writing multi-part arrangements with homophonic passages, following the rules of traditional voice leading will naturally create parts that move in stepwise motion and favor common tones. The part with the most common tones will be easier to play and is appropriate for slower-moving students. For any homophonic music in more than two parts, there should be more students playing the melody than the other parts so the melody is more noticeable. Though homophonic music is easier for an ensemble, polyphony makes it easier to hear the separate parts and is often more musically interesting. Devices like canon and call-and-response work particularly well.

Once students are comfortable in the realm of transposable fingerings (chords that involve fretting all strings), there are no especially difficult keys on the ukulele because students can move the chord formations they know to anywhere on the neck. But when trying to utilize chords (and melodies) containing as many open strings as possible, there are certain keys on the ukulele that involve simpler fingering than others. C major and closely related keys tend to be the simplest in C6 tuning. Keys that are difficult to play in using open strings include C-sharp/D-flat, D-sharp/E-flat, F-sharp/G-flat, and G-sharp/A-flat. See the appendix for a list of chords using only the first five frets and the maximum number of open strings.

Using notation software to create printed materials for students is advisable over handwritten parts, as it is clearer for students and also easier to work with (the major notation programs can generate ukulele chord diagrams, in addition to having the cut/copy/paste features that make for convenient editing). Ukulele music may contain standard notation, strum notation, tablature, chord diagrams, and lyrics, but not all are always appropriate or necessary for a given piece of music. Choosing which components to include depends on the nature of the music itself as well as the learning goals for students. For example, tablature may help make it clearer how a melodic part should be played, but for students who have not mastered reading the treble clef it may look confusingly similar and best be avoided. In this case, chord diagrams would be a better choice to show how to play specific notes. Similarly, a song with a ukulele part consisting entirely of chords but played in specific rhythms at specific times might feature strum notation and chord diagrams for the ukulele accompanied by lyrics and standard notation for the voice.

CHORD "TRICKS"

One of the many ways the ukulele is highly rewarding is that, often, learning one particular chord formation makes it possible to play several different chords. This is because there are usually several different possible formations for the same chord, and identical formations can be used for chords that are

enharmonic equivalents. In some of these formations certain notes are elimi-
nated and/or doubled, making them technically "incomplete" but functional
all the same (these may be convenient when a certain voicing is desired or
when other versions of the chord are beyond a student's technical ability).
Students can maximize their versatility by taking advantage of the following:

All Chords with Four Fretted Strings are Transposable—This includes
barre chords as well as chords in which strings are fretted by separate fingers. Once a student has learned the formation for any type of chord using
four fretted strings, it can be transposed to any key by moving it the appropriate number of frets (half steps) on the fretboard.

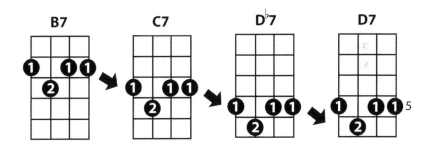

"Power Chords" Can Substitute for Major or Minor Chords—Because
the third is only implied but never heard, power chords may substitute for
major or minor chords at any given time (in certain modal music, they may
even be preferable). There are several possible power chord formations on
the ukulele.

"Power Chords"

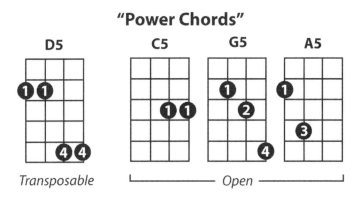

Major Sixth Chords Can Often Substitute for Major Chords—On the ukulele, major sixth chords are usually played with an "added sixth" meaning they include the fifth of the chord. In many cases, these types of sixth chords are simpler or more accessible than the major chord and can be a colorful substitution.

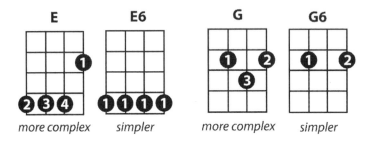

E   E6   G   G6

more complex   *simpler*   *more complex*   *simpler*

Any Diminished Seventh Chord Can Be Played With One of Three Positions—Due to their nature as stacks of minor thirds, the three inversions of any diminished seventh chord are enharmonically equivalent to root position diminished seventh chords in other keys. Thus, only three different chord positions cover all diminished seventh chords (disregarding inversions).

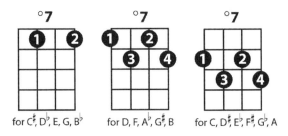

°7   °7   °7

for C♯, D♭, E, G, B♭   for D, F, A♭, G♯, B   for C, D♯, E♭, F♯, G♭, A

Any Augmented Chords Can Be Played with One of Four Positions—Due to their nature as stacks of major thirds, the two inversions of any augmented chord are enharmonically equivalent to root position augmented chords in other keys. Thus, only four different chord positions cover all augmented chords (disregarding inversions).

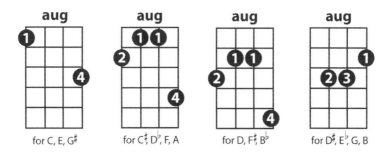

for C, E, G♯　　for C♯, D♭, F, A　　for D, F♯, B♭　　for D♯, E♭, G, B

All Major Sixth Chords Are Minor Seventh Chords—Their "added sixth" quality also makes major sixth chords enharmonically equivalent to their relative minor seventh chord.

All Minor Sixth Chords Can Function as Ninth Chords—Minor sixth chords, like major sixth chords, are played on the ukulele with a sixth added to the regular triad. Since it is impossible to play every pitch of a ninth chord using only four strings, the minor sixth chord provides the necessary pitches for the ninth chords a perfect fourth lower.

ACCOMPANIMENT

A ukulele ensemble may perform independently without accompaniment; however, since all of the instruments in the group are of the same range and tone, the addition of instrument(s) with *bass* can dramatically enhance the sound. A single bass player—whether the teacher or another student— is the most economical choice, though piano/keyboard or even guitar(s) can work as well. The addition of a bassline can also provide rhythmic contrast and create more complex harmonies by modifying the root of the chord. Drums or wind instruments—particularly brass and saxophones— should only be used sparingly or in small numbers with ukuleles, as they can easily drown out the sound.

PROMOTING THE PROGRAM

Since ukuleles are often found in performance only one or two at a time in popular culture (the Ukulele Orchestra of Great Britain notwithstanding), many people may be unfamiliar with the sight and sound of an all-ukulele ensemble. As the school performance may be their first experience with one, and since expectations for ukulele performance in general tend to be low (for better or worse), this has the potential of making the audience all the easier to impress! Teachers should thus take the opportunity to engage the audience, however large or small, and give students the opportunity to do the same, be it through introductions, demonstrations, or solos. Concerts and recitals are prime opportunities to generate positive publicity among the entire school community. An energized student performance is at once the best recruitment tool for new students who want to learn the ukulele and likewise the best way to garner administrative support for continuing or expanding music education with the ukulele and beyond.

APPENDIX

ONE- AND TWO-CHORD SONGS

The following is a sample of songs (*many* more exist) with two chords or less that would be suitable for school usage with little or no adaptation necessary. The suggested keys take into account the range of the melody as well as the simplicity of the necessary chords. Bear in mind that the law prohibits arranging, modifying, reproducing, distributing, or performing copyrighted works without permission (with exceptions for demonstrations by the teacher in the classroom and excerpts that do not constitute a performable unit). Some songs have a popular performer of the song listed for reference purposes, though this is not necessarily the songwriter.

Many one-chord songs can be performed as rounds and all can be played by people who have just learned how to strum the ukulele. Two-chord songs are ideal for beginner ear training and improvisation exercises, as there are only two possible chord changes (with three-chord songs the number of possible changes jumps to six).

Title (Artist)	Genre	Sug. Key(s)	Chords
The Farmer in the Dell	Folk	C	I
Frère Jacques	Folk	C, F	I
Make New Friends	Folk	C, F	I
Row, Row, Row Your Boat	Folk	C	I
Three Blind Mice	Folk	C	I
Coconut (Harry Nilsson)	Pop	C*	I7
Exodus (Bob Marley)	Reggae	Am*	I
Chain of Fools (Aretha Franklin)	Soul	C*	I7
Mary Ann (Roaring Lion)	Calypso	C, F	I, V7
The Banana Boat Song (Harry Belafonte)	Calypso	C	I, V7
Jambalaya (On the Bayou) [Hank Williams]	Country	C	I, V7
Deep In The Heart of Texas (Gene Autry)	Country	F	I, V7
1, 2, 3, 4, 5, 6, 7, 8 (Woody Guthrie)	Folk	F	I, V7
Alouette	Folk	F	I, V7
Going Over the Sea	Folk	F	I, V7
Everybody Loves Saturday Night	Folk	F	I, V7
London Bridge	Folk	C, F	I, V7
The More We Get Together	Folk	C, F	I, V7
Old Joe Clark	Folk	D	I, bVII
Old MacDonald	Folk	F	I, V7
Skip To My Lou	Folk	C, F	I, V7
Rock Island Line	Folk	F	I, V7
Shortenin' Bread	Folk	C	I, V7
Simple Gifts	Folk	F	I, V7
Singin' in the Rain (Gene Kelly)	Mus. Theater	F	I6, ii6
So Long, Farewell (von Trapp Family)	Mus. Theater	C, F	I, V7
Iko Iko (The Dixie Cups)	Pop	C, F	I, V7
Low Rider (War)	Pop	F, G*	I, v
Paperback Writer (The Beatles)	Pop	C, G*	I7, IV7
Everyday People (Sly & The Family Stone)	Soul	G	I, IV
Little Birdie (Vince Guaraldi)	Soul	C, D	I, bVII

*Same key as original recording

CHORDS FOR BEGINNERS

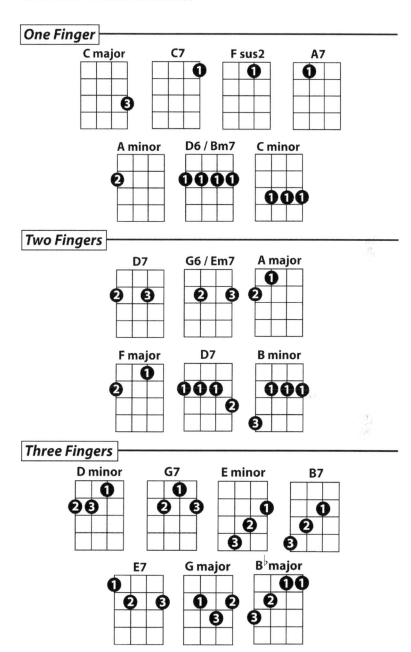

CHORDS FOR BEGINNERS (MODIFIED)

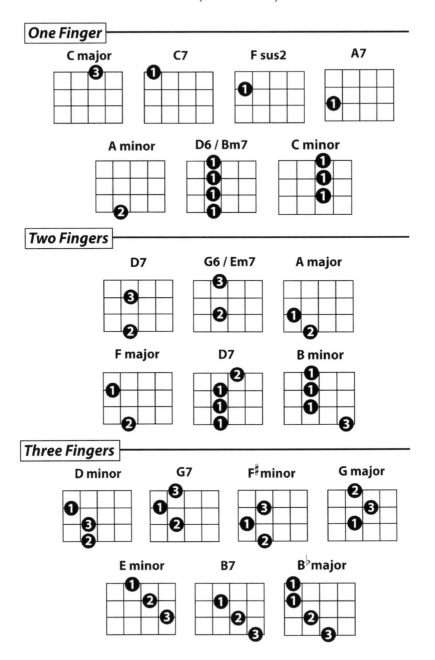

SCALES

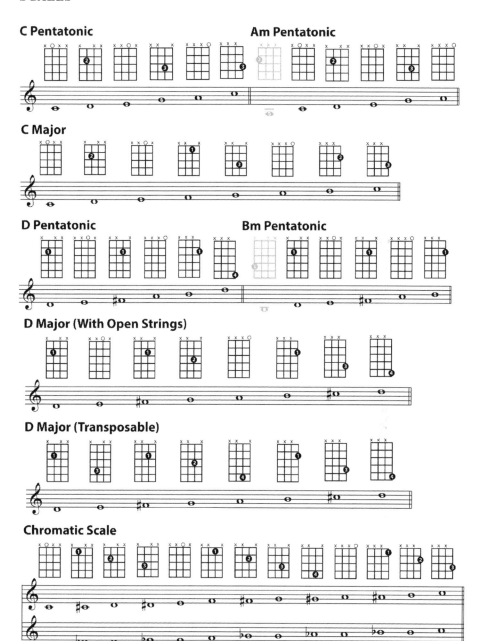

C Pentatonic

Am Pentatonic

C Major

D Pentatonic

Bm Pentatonic

D Major (With Open Strings)

D Major (Transposable)

Chromatic Scale

150 UKULELE CHORDS

There are often many different positions that can be used to produce the same chord on the ukulele, and chords in the same position can sometimes be played with alternative fingerings. This chart represents only chord positions that are located in the first five frets and use the maximum possible number of open strings. The suggested fingering is based on comfort and common usage.

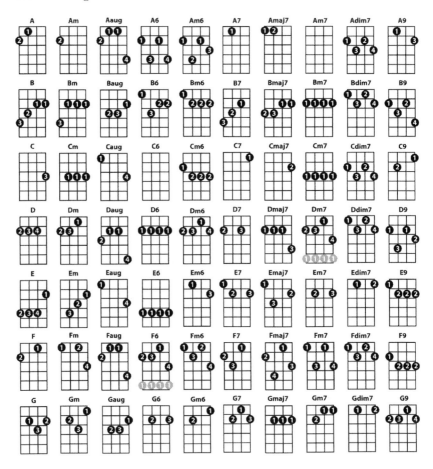

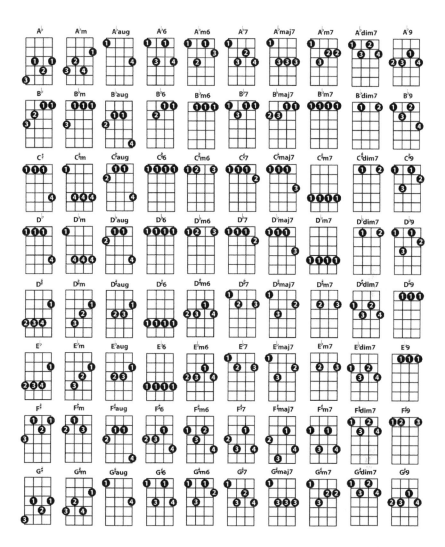

GLOSSARY

Barre (v.)—Left-hand technique that involves using a finger to press on several strings at once in the same fret.

Barre Chord—A chord involving one finger pressing across several strings at once in the same fret.

Body—The hollow lower portion of the ukulele in which sound resonates.

Bridge—The raised structure on the body of the ukulele below the sound hole; it contains the lower anchor point of the strings.

Chord Diagram—A form of notation in which a grid representing the strings and frets of the ukulele shows where fingers should be placed to play a particular chord.

Chord Formation—The arrangement of the fingers for a chord position, regardless of location on the fretboard.

Chord Position—The exact location of the fingers on the fretboard needed to play a specific chord.

Fret (n.) *or* **Fret Wire**—The raised metal band on the fretboard that shortens the vibrating area of the string when a finger is pressed behind it.

Fret (v.)—The act of pressing a string into the space between two neighboring fret wires (or the nut).

Fretboard *or* **Fingerboard**—The top surface of the neck, sometimes extending onto the top surface of the body, containing all frets.

Fret Marker—Inlay markings on the fretboard in specific frets, indicating where common intervals relative to pitches of the open strings are located.

Fretted Note—A note requiring the string to be pressed into a fret.

Fretted String—A string whose vibrating area is shortened by pressing it into a particular fret.

Head *or* **Headstock**—The top portion of the ukulele where the strings are anchored and from which they may be tuned.

Lead Sheet—A piece of sheet music containing only a melody (including any lyrics) and chord names.

Neck—The middle portion of the ukulele connecting the head and the body.

Nut—The notched band holding the strings in place at the top of the fretboard.

Open String—A string played without fretting.

Picking *or* **Fingerpicking**—Using the thumb and finger(s) to pluck strings.

Saddle—The raised part of the bridge over which the strings pass before being attached to the bridge itself.

Soundboard—The front face of the ukulele body.

Sound Hole—The hole in the body underneath the strings from which reverberated sound projects.

Strumming—Using the thumb or finger(s) to brush across several strings in one motion.

Sustain—The degree to which sound continues after a string is plucked or strummed.

Tablature—System of notation containing four horizontal lines, representing the strings of the ukulele, with numbers placed on the lines indicating which fret to hold while picking or strumming. Read from left to right, with vertical stacking of simultaneously sounded pitches.

Tuner *or* **Tuning Peg**—The mechanism used for tightening or loosening a string to change the pitch.

INDEX

Made in the USA
Monee, IL
27 October 2020

46169601R00074